Breaking the Press The Incredible Story of the All American Red Heads

Breaking the Press The Incredible Story of the All American Red Heads

• • •

Orwell Moore and Tammy Moore Harrison
With Howard Rankin

Breaking the Press
©2016 Tammy Moore Harrison & Orwell Moore & Howard Rankin

ISBN-13: 9780692798263
ISBN-10: 0692798269

Printed in the United States
Available from Amazon.com and other retail outlets

Acknowledgments

● ● ●

I WOULD LIKE TO THANK the many people who helped make this book possible. First my husband, Johnny Harrison, who has put up with my preoccupation with the Red Heads for years. He has allowed me to turn a room of our home into a storage and sorting area filled with years of Red Heads memorabilia.

To my daughter, Cassie Nelson, who helped me with social media, proofread all of my letters and notes, traveled to events, and designed the cover of this book. Colby Harrison, my son, for helping me over the years organizing all of the information that had to be gone though and also for being my date to some of the important Red Heads events.

To all of the team members and coaches of the All American Red Heads, I have a special appreciation and gratitude for you all. You have provided me with spectacular memories to write about! To those of you and your families who have attended events and reunions throughout the years, thank you for keeping the team together and the memories alive. Without your continued commitment and love for Red Heads basketball, this story might have been forgotten. To single out specific individuals would be too difficult of a task. For those of you who showed your support and respect toward my parents and family—you know who you are—thank you from the bottom of my heart.

To all the players, coaches, and managers recognized in the back of this book, the phrase "It takes a village" does not encapsulate the true meaning of what we have all accomplished. For us, it is better said this way: "It takes a team."

Most of all I want to express my sincere thanks to my mother and father, who spent their lives loving and living the Red Heads. You taught me many things in life. Thank you for sharing this with me.

And finally, Howard Rankin, I am not sure if this book would have been born without you agreeing to take on and complete this project. Sifting through years of fragmented information in disorganized boxes was indeed a project; with that said, you were able to finish my father's words and capture the persona and history of the All American Red Heads through my father's eyes. And, if I must say, you did so beautifully...as they deserve.

Contents

Acknowledgments · v
Foreword ·ix

Chapter 1   Hall of Fame · 1
Chapter 2   Play, Not Competition · 4
Chapter 3   Ole Olson and the Terrible Swedes · · · · · · · · · · · · · · · 9
Chapter 4   1930s The Legend Begins · 15
Chapter 5   1945–1954 The Legend Resumes · · · · · · · · · · · · · · · 26
Chapter 6   1955–1960 The Legend Expands · · · · · · · · · · · · · · · 37
Chapter 7   A Day on the Road · 48
Chapter 8   Who Are the Red Heads? · 54
Chapter 9   The Swinging Sixties · 63
Chapter 10   Basketball: The Magnificent Game · · · · · · · · · · · · · · 75
Chapter 11   Camp Courage · 79
Chapter 12   The Sparkling Seventies · 84
Chapter 13   The Evolving Eighties · 93
Chapter 14   Reunions · 100
Chapter 15   A Family Affair · 105
Chapter 16   The Dream Is Realized · 111
Chapter 17   The Ultimate Prize · 113
Chapter 18   All American Red Heads Players and Coaches · · · · · · · · 116

About the Authors · 137

Foreword

● ● ●

As far back as I can remember, my life has been filled with red, white, blue, basketball, and the All American Red Heads. The talented Red Heads personnel were not just employees of my family but family members. Sometimes they would just drop by during the off-season or after their playing days were over. My parents received letters and phone calls regularly from both current and past players offering updates on their lives, asking about the team, or simply checking in.

Rehab clinics didn't exist during the Red Heads era to the extent they do now. Despite all of the training, with sports, injuries happened. When a player was impacted by an injury, he or she would often recuperate at my family's home. In some cases, it was for an extended period of time.

My brother, Burnie, and I spent our vacations traveling to and watching basketball games. It was during these times when I actually got to know the ladies beyond their basketball personas. Even though their "characters" were built around their actual personalities, the real women, away from the court, were the true inspirations. From a very young age, I traveled a lot with the team. We did everything together: ate, talked, sang, played cards, visited the tourist sites, and played pranks on each other. We would also scout out new recruits and attend sports conferences. I have to admit, it was quite an exciting life.

When I reached the age of twelve, traveling became harder because of school and social activities. I still had opportunities to travel with the team but stayed for shorter lengths of time. During the winter months, the Red

Heads were usually scheduled to play in the western part of the county. This was definitely my favorite place to visit, because it was so beautiful to me.

One thing that wasn't so easy to find when traveling was food. During our travels those days, there wasn't a gas station or fast-food restaurant every few miles or blocks. This made finding a place to stop and eat extremely difficult, especially when we traveled as a large group. Many of the towns had only one restaurant, and on nights we had games, we had to request that they stay open later than their regular hours if we anticipated our game might run past its scheduled finish.

Summer months were spent making preparations for the following seasons. This was the most important part of the year for my parents. They were reviewing scouting notes to hire players, booking games, sending out marketing materials, doing public relations, completing uniform and equipment inventory, and, I am certain, attending to more tasks than I can remember. My mother often made and repaired the uniforms. I helped my parents with the day-to-day business of operating the Red Heads, such as organizing and keeping inventory of the marketing materials and posters. I also helped my parents by mailing letters to venues in order to promote the team and/or schedule games. My friend Diane used to help out as much as she could, so we were able to play sooner. This was before answering machines, caller ID, and fax machines, and I had my work cut out for me answering the seemingly endless phone calls. That phone would ring at all hours of the night and day! Eventually, it became evident we needed two phones lines, one for business and one for personal.

During this time, business-related road trips were not only a necessity, but they were also required of my parents and the coaching staff. The crowd consisted of my uncle Jack and aunt Bettye, Bettye's brothers and sisters, and Pat and Ben Overman. We would all pile into the All American Red Heads' limo (currently displayed at the Women's Basketball Hall of Fame in Knoxville), so we could travel more comfortably together. We would watch high school all-star games and attend coaches' conferences.

I loved going on these trips not only for the basketball games but also for the family time that we all spent together.

Spring training took place in Caraway, Arkansas. Many players had to fly to training camp. The closest airport was in Memphis, which was an hour away. Caraway was a very small town, and there were no hotels close, so the girls stayed with us or in nearby towns.

At camp, there was the ritual we called the "dyeing of the hair." Miss Clairol, Flame Red, is the color I remember. My mother, Aunt Bettye, and veteran players would suit up for the occasion. Their uniforms included rubber gloves, old clothes, aprons, and a bottle of hair dye. Hair coloring was not as prevalent or as simple as it is today. This was most girls' first experience in having their natural hair color changed. Today people change their hair color with the seasons but not at that time. Most people were shocked the first time they looked in the mirror. Could you yourself imagine going from black, blond, or brown hair—and in a blink of an eye having Flame Red hair?

The next part of the ritual was the attire. The uniform needed to be made and fitted. My mother sewed and fitted the uniforms, purchased tennis shoes, and arranged for the players to have their pictures taken at Child Art Studio in Paragould, Arkansas. After all this prep work was done, the players were then ready to get down to the business of basketball and what it meant to be an All American Red Head. My dad and the other coaches spent many hours a day on conditioning, teaching the plays, practicing the tricks and stunts, and focusing on the mental aspect of the game.

Summers were spent in Caraway until Camp Courage was purchased. From then on, the summers were spent there. This meant training moved from Caraway to Holley Springs, Mississippi. The first year, there was only one cabin on the lake that was habitable. Everybody had to stay there. It was wall-to-wall beds. The hair dyeing, uniform fitting, and other mustdos to start the season happened there.

If there wasn't a scrimmage or a practice, we would watch television or play cards. Eventually, more cabins and spaces were built. Camp Courage had three cabins, a large outdoor basketball court, a bathhouse, a mess hall (cafeteria), a swimming pool, tennis courts, a sauna room, and an athletic whirlpool. It was definitely a top-of-the-line type of camp. My mom or Miss Carolyn usually cooked for everyone. It was pretty rustic there. Being in the woods with nothing but lakes or trees around is one of my favorite childhood memories.

The first Red Heads reunion was in Jonesboro, Arkansas, in 1996. I did not know what to expect. It had been years since I last saw most of the ladies. By this time, most had started families or moved to the opposite side of the country. This was the first time my kids—Cassie, in high school, and Colby, around three—had met the players. As you will read, the turnout was so amazing and everyone had such a great time, it ended up starting somewhat of a tradition. It was a rewarding event for my family.

It was so wonderful to hear how much playing for the Red Heads had meant to these women. Many of the ladies had heard stories about players who came before them, and it was rewarding for them to have a chance to meet them. I, for one, was blessed with knowing each and every one of them. It was interesting to have the opportunity to revisit them as an adult rather than a child or a teenager. I also enjoyed getting to know their families and sharing my memories of their loved ones. As the reunions continued, the feeling of being part of a bigger basketball picture became evident. This brought great joy to my mom, dad, and me. Hearing players talk about how the Red Heads changed their lives made me feel as though my parents had made such a dramatic difference. After each reunion, I could feel the fellowships strengthening as well.

Being a part of Red Heads basketball continues to bless me today. It goes far beyond basketball. Being a part of the Red Heads family has enriched my life in many ways. I was fortunate enough to be able to travel, meet wonderful people, and participate in activities like the Sears Salute to Champions and both the men's and women's Basketball Halls of Fame. I am overwhelmed to know that I have lived such a blessed life. It sometimes takes growing up and having family members and friends pass to notice.

I am thankful for every minute I have spent with the wonderful group of men and women who helped shape the history of basketball.

And now I am delighted to share my story with you.

Tammy Moore Harrison
May 2016

Dedicated to : Orwell and Lorene Moore

CHAPTER 1

Hall of Fame

● ● ●

A winner is someone who recognizes his God-given talents, works his tail
off to develop them into skills, and uses these skills to accomplish his goals.

—LARRY BIRD

WE WERE ABOUT TO WALK on the stage. I was there with many of my
friends, familiar faces with whom I shared memories stretching back more
than fifty years. In many ways they were my family. This was going to be
the biggest public speech I would ever make, and it was in front of a room
filled with household names, all global sporting icons in their own rights.
It was also being filmed and broadcast live.

Julius Erving, the unmistakable Dr. J, escorted me onto the platform.
He had told me that he had seen the Red Heads play when he was in
school, and he was honored to lead me onto basketball's greatest stage.
There was a standing ovation as first I, then the former Red Heads players
and coaches, made our way into the spotlight.

I took my place at the podium and looked briefly around at all the celebrities who were waiting for me to speak. It was an honor but also a responsibility. I wanted to ensure that I paid appropriate respect to all the people
who had led up to me being on the stage at this precise incredible moment.

"Thank you for honoring us."

The people most on my mind as I stood at the podium were my mother
and father, extraordinary influences and the main reasons I was standing

there. Basketball and the All-American Red Heads had been my parents' lives. My father, Orwell Moore, coached and then owned the team for more than thirty years. My mother, Lorene Moore, played on the team and scored more than thirty-five thousand points!

"My mom, the leading all-time scorer. Can you imagine that? Kareem, you have nothing on my mom."

My dad had a complete understanding of the game, a gift for anticipating future coaching methods, and a brilliant marketing mind. He found a way to combine athleticism and entertainment in a unique way, allowing women to step outside the stereotypes of the times.

"Basketball is a simple game; you need a ball and a hoop—and, oh, the opportunity to play, of course. During this time the opportunities for women were incredibly limited. It was considered socially unacceptable and physically impossible to run up and down the floor, to sweat and to compete. The woman's place was in the home."

My parents lived the game and the Red Heads, and so did I.

"I can't remember life without the All American Red Heads in it, nor would I want to."

As I briefly recounted the history of the Red Heads, I talked about C. M. Ole Olson and his wife, Doyle, who started the whole thing back in the 1930s. I mentioned Ole's love of basketball, flair for creativity, and knack for gimmicks.

"Do you know that Olson was the first man to throw a behind-the-back pass—so, Magic, you might just owe Ole a high five for all those magical passes you made."

Ole was definitely way ahead of the times. It takes someone like that to start a revolution.

"He put them in shiny uniforms, dyed their hair red, taught them all the tricks in the book, and—oh yeah, scheduled their games against men's teams."

But Ole and Doyle, my father and my mother, and all of those associated with the Red Heads didn't just play basketball—they changed a stereotype and paved the way for future generations of women to participate and become champions in their own rights.

"Ole and Doyle broke the ice and gave women a future in sports."

Yes, here I was accepting the honor of the All American Red Heads being pioneers not just in this sport of basketball but in sport in general.

"Just think—the first women's basketball team to be inducted into the Naismith Hall of Fame."

The Red Heads were a phenomenon that spanned half a century. They played as many as two hundred games a year, as far afield as Alaska, Canada, Mexico, and the Philippines. They once had a ninety-six-game winning streak. At one point they were so popular that they had three teams touring the country. They packed out gyms across the country and became models for a different sort of female role.

"They thrilled the fans with fancy passes, crazy ball handling, deceptive play patterns, clever ruses, amusing routines, and great basketball."

The story you are about to read is about how two couples who loved basketball were able to change not just a game but a perception about the capabilities of women. The fact that I was at the podium accepting the honor was a testimony to the importance of that idea and the extent to which they, and all those associated with the Red Heads, had succeeded.

It all started 120 years earlier, when basketball itself was conceived as the game we know today.

CHAPTER 2

Play, Not Competition

● ● ●

*The battle for the individual rights of women is one of long standing
and none of us should countenance anything which undermines it.*

—ELEANOR ROOSEVELT

THE WOMEN ON THE COURT were playing a game newly invented by a guy
called Naismith. The girls were playing by their own rules, which they had
recently adapted. The baskets were enclosed and fashioned after wastebas-
kets. The ball was a soccer ball. There were no backboards. There were
three sections to the court. The back section was just for the guards, who
couldn't actually guard or try to steal the ball. The front section was for
the forwards, the only ones who could shoot. Dribbling was restricted,
and no one could hold the ball for more than three seconds. There were
six women on the court for each team at any one time, although in some
variations there could be as many as eleven players a side. Only one-
handed shots were allowed, and players could only run when the ball was
in the air. This was almost a century before Magic and Kareem and almost
thirty years before women got to vote. This was the world of basquette in
the early 1890s, which had taken James Naismith's recently created game
of basketball and converted it for women.

One of the people instrumental in raising the profile of basketball
for women came from an unlikely background. Senda Berenson, an

immigrant from Lithuania, settled with her family in Boston when she was seven years old. From all accounts, Senda was frail and in poor health, which prevented her from fully pursuing her artistic and musical interests, and she seemed like the least likely person to promote women's sports. Ironically, her health issues were what brought her into contact with the noncontact sport.

The unwinding story is testimony to the value of being in the right place at the right time and impressing the right people. It starts with Mary Hemenway, a Boston philanthropist who opened numerous schools in the reconstructed South and was all about education and self-improvement. In 1888 she introduced Boston-area schoolteachers to a physical-education program used in Sweden, a country that would figure prominently in the early part of this story. In 1889 Hemenway arranged a conference on physical training that some say impacted the whole concept of physical education in American schools. At this point in the story we are introduced to Amy Morris Homans, who, having worked in some of those southern schools mentioned above, met Hemenway and became her executive secretary. It was Homans who organized that 1889 physical-training conference.

That same year Hemenway opened the Boston Normal School of Gymnastics (which later became part of Wellesley College), and Amy Homans became the first director. There were several notables on the faculty from Harvard and from the Royal Central Institute of Gymnastics founded in Sweden.

Senda Berenson found out about the school, applied, and was accepted despite the fact that she did not have the required high school graduation certificate and, perhaps more importantly, was in poor physical shape. Homans, however, saw Berenson's potential; she was sure that the physical activities would improve Berenson's health, thus proving the value of the program both to Berenson and others.

Homans was right.

Initially, Berenson hated the physical challenge, but she stuck with it, started to improve, and by the end of the year was doing the recommended two hours of exercise a day and reaping the benefits. She was converted.

Homans was so impressed with Berenson that she gave her the task of teaching the faculty of a school in Andover about the Swedish gymnastics method. Berenson did such a good job that when an opening became available to teach gymnastics at the all-female Smith College, Homans heartily endorsed her, even though Senda had yet to finish her two-year course. And that's how Senda Berenson ended up in the right place at the right time to adapt Naismith's new game of basketball and develop it for women.

In the 1890s, the notion that women should be involved in physical activities and sports was not commonly held. Women were seen as weaker and more vulnerable. For example, a significant number of women were still dying in childbirth. Although the United States did not keep maternal mortality rates until 1915, the experience of almost all advanced countries was the same; mortality rates in childbirth remained high throughout the latter part of the nineteenth century and only started a dramatic decline in the 1930s. What is also interesting is that during this time and even prior to it, infant mortality rates were related to class, with the poorer children having the highest death rates. But where records of these factors were kept, specifically in Great Britain, the evidence suggested that the reverse was true for maternal mortality rates; the higher the social standing, the greater the mortality risk. The fact was that the British upper classes had money and access to doctors, who, it turns out, weren't as good as midwives at keeping moms alive during delivery.

In addition, the woman's place was in the home, according to the values of the times. Certainly up until this point in time, the prevailing view had been that women's roles revolved around family and the home, while men were seen as wage earners and very definitely the heads of the household. However, with more women becoming college graduates, there was a movement to end these gender stereotypes—although in the 1890s this really hadn't yet changed the perception of the role of women. The genders were by no means equal.

This was the context in which Berenson tried to introduce mandatory physical education for female students. She had to convince the skeptical faculty, but she did indeed get physical exercise on to the regular curriculum at Smith, which was an achievement in itself.

At Smith she found herself in a school with excellent and newly updated physical-fitness facilities, including a new gym. Fueled by her own personal experience of the benefits of exercise, Berenson taught classes in the Swedish gymnastics method to the female students. Although Berenson was enthusiastic, she discovered much to her surprise that many of the students were not. She looked for other ways of engaging the girls in physical activities.

Berenson had read about Naismith's new game of basketball, and it was one of a number of games she introduced to make the concept of physical activity more engaging to her students. Women playing any kind of sport was a novel idea back at the end of the nineteenth century. Berenson introduced the game at class level and got such a good response from the students that she organized an interclass game, sophomores against freshmen. The sophomores won the first competitive game of women's basketball, which was watched by an all-women crowd—no men were allowed.

Women's basketball had been born, and over the next few years Berenson devised rules specifically for women, some of which were designed to minimize what Berenson saw as a "tendency towards roughness."[1] Although Berenson enjoyed the friendly competition, her main goal was to use basketball as a way to get her students in good physical shape. She was more concerned with the physical activity and the fun of playing than with competition per se. Moreover, she saw the activity in the context of students' overall education. Students could not play if they were failing classes, and Berenson stressed the overall educational value of the game, a theme that will be repeated later in the story.

Women's basketball began to spread. In 1896, the first intercollegiate game was played on the West Coast between Stanford and Berkeley, and games were reported for the first time in the states of Washington and

1 Melnick, Ralph (2007). *Senda Berenson: The Unlikely Founder of Women's Basketball.* Amherst: University of Massachusetts Press.

Illinois. A great timeline of women's basketball can be found at https://womenshoopsblog.wordpress.com/, which traces the development of the sport, including the fact that in 1899, "Stanford's faculty athletic committee rules that women can no longer compete at the intercollegiate level. Soon Cal follows suit."

Berenson had been extremely influential in helping establish the game for women. It now faced the challenge of being accepted, a challenge that would unfold over the next eight decades.

Berenson had reached basketball by a circuitous route, which was heavily influenced by Swedish gymnastics. And a Swede was going to feature in another major development in the women's basketball game.

CHAPTER 3

Ole Olson and the Terrible Swedes

● ● ●

What you are as a person is far more important
than what you are as a basketball player.

—JOHN WOODEN

THERE'S A STORY ABOUT C. M. "Connie Mack" Olson that happened almost a hundred years ago. He was playing baseball and did something that displeased the umpire. The umpire fined him fifteen dollars and told him he was banned from playing until he paid the fine. The next day, Olson turned up to play, and on his first at bat came to the plate with a bag. He emptied the bag, which contained fifteen hundred pennies, at the feet of the umpire.

That story says a lot about C. M. Olson. He was athletic, innovative, fearless, independent, and competitive, and all of those qualities were a critical part of what shaped Olson's contribution to basketball in general and women's sports in particular.

In the first part of the twentieth century, there were no computers, cell phones, or even televisions. Everyone had to entertain himself or herself and had the time to do so. For young adults this meant playing sports on makeshift courts, diamonds, and fields. In the cities and in rural areas, young people were active and creative. Not only did this mean that young people were physically active and engaged in sports, it also provided the opportunity for some enterprising people to make money from barnstorming—going from community to community to play exhibition games against local opposition.

In the 1920s immigrants were still arriving in vast numbers, and there emerged the second generation of those who had arrived in America since the end of the last century. Moreover, these immigrants, while slowly integrating into American society, still identified with their ethnic origins and lived in communities that defined their heritage. So it was no surprise that sports teams and even leagues developed around these national and ethnic groups. In towns and in rural areas, young adults played ball, organized around their cultural identities.

In this environment, promoters with an entrepreneurial spirit recognized the opportunity to turn athletic competition into a profit. For example, there was a group of black basketball players at Wendell Phillips High School on the south side of Chicago who formed themselves into a team called the Globetrotters. Soon afterward, their new promoter and manager, Abe Saperstein, had them touring the state. Saperstein knew that they had to have a catchy name and, in recognition of the role and association that Harlem had with black culture, renamed them the Harlem Globetrotters. It would be more than forty years before the Globetrotters actually played a game in Harlem.

Baseball, horseback riding, and boxing were the most popular sports. In basketball, in addition to the Harlem Globetrotters, there were famous teams like the Buffalo Germans, the New York Celtics, and the South Philadelphia Hebrew Association. Basketball was promoted by the YMCA, and many games were played there.

Before the advent of household television, if you wanted to see sports you had to actually go to a game and watch the action live. As a result, barnstorming was popular in both baseball and basketball. If you wanted to watch, there was a game near you pitting local teams made up of people in your community, like teachers and shopkeepers, against touring opposition. Moreover, the barnstorming teams made money by charging for admission to games (around fifty cents), and so these teams were part athletic endeavor, part business. And some teams became very popular and very successful.

It was against this backdrop that in 1920, C. M. Olson formed his own basketball team in Coffeyville, Kansas. They were called the Terrible Swedes. The adjective must have been identified with the nationality, because there was also a baseball team in Andover, New Hampshire, by the same name. Around this time there was also a family basketball team consisting of five brothers and two sisters called the Flying Swedes. But it was Olson's Kansas-based Terrible Swedes that got the attention.

According to Paul Johns's column entitled "Mozark Moments" and dated March 2012, available at ccheadliner.com, his research led him to this statement in an article in the *Elmira Gazette* dated January 12, 1920: "the Swedes had beaten another team 33 to 18."

Reports of games and other information can be found on different parts of the Internet. Posting on the website www.apbr.org, a gentleman with the unforgettable screen name Dementia Man provided details of games played by the Swedes, information apparently gained while the author was researching the Harlem Globetrotters. The author wrote that, "within a decade, the Swedes—with two units in some seasons—had become the premier basketball attraction in the western and middle western states." The author suggests that the Swedes were no match for the New York Celtics, who dominated in the East, and Olson's team "often struggled against local amateur sides." However, Olson was recognized as "a good showman and top ballyhoo artist." Those teams barnstorming for money realized that they had to provide more than just a game; they knew that they were in the entertainment business. Being a showman, promoter, and "ballyhoo artist" were prerequisites for success.

Reports of games included a 1925 game against the Oakland Knights of Columbus, in which the Swedes lost by two points; a nail-biter of a game in Marion, Ohio, in 1926, in which the Swedes nipped the Isaly Dairies 35–34; and a discouraging game in Beloit, Wisconsin, in which the Swedes lost to the hometown Beloit Fairies, 44–35. Other games in 1934 were reported against college teams: Washington State College, Willamette, and San Diego State. In the game against San Diego State, a team led by none other than Art Linkletter, the Swedes won 29–23, and the *San Diego Union* newspaper reported the following:

"Olson generally is considered the greatest back-handed passer in the game, and his comic antics on the court have won him acclaim throughout the Swedes' current nationwide tour. He has a good running mate to aid him in his work as comedian, diminutive Dutch Richeson being a master clown and player. Richeson and Olson bounced the ball off their heads, fired backward passes and did everything but pull burning cigars out of their jerseys."

The *San Diego Union* also reported this about the Swedes: "In addition to guards Ed Grant and Wayne Howdyshell and veteran captain-center Gus Babb, over the past 13 years, the team claims to have performed before 1,000,000 fans."

Olson knew that the West and the Midwest were fertile grounds for a barnstorming basketball team and claimed that the attendances at games at these locations could draw ten times the number of people at games played elsewhere in the country. Being a touring team obviously paid off for Olson. The *San Diego Union* wrote the following:

"The Swedes won 120 games last year, losing just 8, and had a run of 60 straight victories during their unmarred invasion of the west. They appeared in California, Utah, Idaho, Wyoming, New Mexico, Colorado, Texas, Indiana, Louisiana, Georgia, Alabama, Arkansas, Tennessee, Illinois, Oklahoma, Kentucky, Iowa and other states. They defeated 16 college and university teams last year and received 2,300 applications for games and they will play in almost every state before the present tour expires," wrote the San Diego Union.

Dementia Man also includes information from the Swedes' 1934–35 publicity guide, which heralds "a virtually all new team with 6-10 Art (Big Boy) Stoelting joining the club." The press guide goes on to promote the team:

"The Swedes have an original style of play, using a minimum of effort and relying on unorthodox passes to work the ball down the court. The frog dribble, back-handed pass and other such spectacular maneuvers are a part of the Olson routine and the barnstormers even have been known to butt the ball through the webbing with their heads."

Olson and his wife, Doyle, had moved to Cassville, Missouri, in 1933, and C. M.'s coaching and playing days were coming to an end—at least for the Swedes. However, Olson was not just a creative player and coach; he was also a tough businessman.

An unidentified source in Great Falls, Montana, writing on February 2, 1935, wrote the following:

It is reported here that C. M. Olson, owner and manager of Olson's Terrible Swedes and a new traveling negro team, the Harlemites, says he has canceled a scheduled Tuesday night, Feb. 5, game here against the Great Falls Great Northerns. Olson said his contract called for his Harlemites to be the first Afro-American club to play in Great Falls. When he arrived here he discovered that both Pullin's Globe Trotters and Saperstein's original Harlem Globe Trotters had appeared here. The Harlemites played before nearly 2,000 fans at the Anaconda winter carnival; they also had an overflow house at Crow Agency during a recent tour of southern Montana. Olson reports that not a single game has been lost in Montana and Wyoming (as of January 30, 1935). A series of games with the Swedes and southern Montana indy squads are to keep them busy until February 12, when they hit for Dakota country.

It wasn't just trick plays and comic stunts, including free throws shot over his head with his back to the basket, that propelled Olson and the Swedes; they could shoot from long distances too. One report from a Spartanburg, South Carolina, paper recounted Olson's great long shooting on a night in which he scored 18 points in a 44–30 win. Another game program from that time promoted the Swedes as "America's only back hand passing club," and "claimant of the world championship." The program suggests that the Swedes played some of their games at the Union Hi auditorium in Humansville, Kansas.

As Olson and his wife settled in Cassville, Missouri, his playing days were winding down. But his business days were far from over, and his entrepreneurial spirit lived on. It's unclear whether C. M. had a plan for what was next, but anyone who knew him surely realized it would be unconventional, innovative, and on a large scale. After all, Olson was a great ballyhoo artist, and you can't keep a man like that down for long.

CHAPTER 4

1930s
The Legend Begins

● ● ●

How do you go from where you are to where you wanna be? I
think you have to have an enthusiasm for life. You have to have
a dream, a goal. And you have to be willing to work for it.

—JIM VALVANO

CASSVILLE IS A SMALL TOWN in the southwestern corner of Missouri. It is described by its chamber of commerce as a "thriving city nestled in the heart of the Ozarks." A recent census had more than three thousand residents and over eight hundred households registered in the town. Cassville is also the county seat of Barry County, which also has numerous townships and villages. When Ole and Doyle settled there in 1933, they had a plan to service the town, the county, and beyond in both Missouri and Arkansas with a chain of beauty parlors.

Interestingly, the beauty-and hair-salon business was changing as rapidly as the basketball game, and at about the same time. In the late nineteenth century, when Naismith was coming up with the new game, the increase in plumbing and the design of the shampoo bowl brought hairstyling and hair coloring for women into vogue. Around this time, Martha Matilda Harper opened one of the first public salons and invented the now-ubiquitous recliner chair, allowing easier access for hair shampooing and washing. Then in the 1920s, as basketball was gathering popularity as described in the last chapter, the advent of the hairdryer, hair color, and bobby pins led to an explosion of interest in beauty as a business. It is estimated that more than twenty-five thousand salons opened in the 1920s. One can only imagine how the possibilities of this new business appealed to that top ballyhoo artist, C. M. Olson, and his equally sharp wife, Doyle.

So while today we take hair coloring and all the typical aspects of a beauty salon for granted, they really exploded on the scene just a few short years before Ole and Doyle decided to get into that business. In hindsight, it is obvious that for the imaginative and entrepreneurial Olsons, basketball and hair coloring were a match made in henna.

Basketball statistics are one thing, but how about these numbers on hair color, thanks to the Regis Salons website?

* **92 percent:** the number of women who have attempted to color their hair
* **1860:** the year hydrogen peroxide was first used to bleach hair
* **1907:** the year synthetic hair dye was invented
* **20:** the number of minutes one had to simmer crushed marigold flowers to make a rinse that added reddish-gold highlights to hair, according to herbalists of the early 1900s
* **1931:** the year Jean Harlow was described as a platinum blonde in the movie with same name
* **2005:** the year when Roodharigendag (Redhead Day) was started in Holland

Exactly how and when the idea to field a women's basketball team occurred to the Olsons is hard to say. One version of events is that a couple of the girls who worked in the Olsons' salons played basketball, and it was their presence that sparked the imaginative leap to combine beauty and basketball. Or perhaps, given Ole's passion for the game, girls who played the game were given preference for jobs in the salons. Or maybe one or both of the Olsons watched local basketball games and recruited girls for their salons from the players they met.

One thing we do know is that an unmarried beautician named Mama Langerman raised twin daughters who were both basketball stars in Iowa. Jean and Jo Langerman featured in high school state championships in both Parkersburg and Hampton, Iowa. They then went to play for Tulsa Business College Stenographers, who were the AAU 1934 championships. Their mother, who was doing something of a barnstorming beautician tour herself, ended up in Missouri, and before long her daughters were critical parts of the first Red Heads team. Exactly how the Olsons and Langermans met is unclear, but their meeting would be a big step in the successful launch of the Olsons' groundbreaking challenge to convention. In any event, it wasn't too long before the idea of a women's basketball team formed in the minds of the Olsons.

Fielding a women's basketball team was not unique in the mid-1930s. Getting to that point, however, required overcoming some hurdles. For example, in 1908 the Amateur Athletic Union's (AAU) position was that women should not play basketball in public. And in 1914 the American Olympic Committee opposed the notion of women's basketball as an Olympic sport. The tide began to turn a bit during the 1920s, when several companies sponsored women's teams in various industrial leagues. The Jeux Olympique Feminines also staged games featuring sports that women couldn't compete in at the Olympics, including basketball. Before the 1920s were over, however, the Olympics did feature women's basketball—as an exhibition event. But there was still some major opposition. The Women's Division of the National Amateur Athletic Federation (WDNAAF) took the position that basketball, along with other sports, was too competitive for women and launched campaigns to prevent the sport being played in schools, industrial leagues, or frankly anywhere.

According to archived information from the Women's Sports Foundation available at https://raycityhistory.wordpress.com/tag/wdnaaf/, which is dedicated to the history of Ray City, Georgia, one version of these events was characterized like this:

As the game's popularity grew, so did the backlash from educators concerned that the physical activity was unladylike, inappropriate

and unhealthy. This seesaw battle of growth and resistance continued into the early 20's, but the balance shifted in 1923 when
Lou Henry Hoover, head of Girl Scouts of America and wife of
President Herbert Hoover, helped organize the Women's Division
of the National Amateur Athletic Federation (WDNAAF). In
1925, the WDNAAF passed a resolution outlawing extramural
competition, opposing gate-receipts, all travel for women's games
and all publicity of women's sports. The National Association
of Secondary School Principals supported the resolution and
they, in turn, pressured high school sports associations to dis-
band tournaments. By the mid-'30s, competitive basketball at
elementary, high school and college level in many states had all
but disappeared.

The arguments against female athletic competition were well summarized
in Dr. Dudley Sargent's 1912 publication "Are Athletics Making Girls
Masculine? A Practical Answer to a Question Every Girl Asks." Sargent
lays out the problem in the first paragraph like this (warning: this was
written more than a hundred years ago):

"Many persons honestly believe that athletics are making girls bold,
masculine and overassertive; that they are destroying the beautiful lines
and curves of her figure, and are robbing her of that charm and elusive-
ness that has so long characterized the female sex. Others including many
physicians incline to the belief that athletics are injurious to health."

Dr. Sargent then goes on to make the distinction between physical
activity as general "development" and as competition. The former is more
acceptable, the latter far less so. And Sargent makes the distinction between
the physical and psychological consequences of athletic engagement.

"Physically all forms of athletic sports and most physical exercises
tend to make women's figures more masculine," writes Sargent. However,
on the "positive" side, he writes that, "some of the specific mental and
physical qualities which are developed by athletics are increased powers of
attention, will, concentration, accuracy, alertness, quickness of perception,

perseverance, reason, judgment, forbearance, patience, obedience, self-control, loyalty to leaders, self-denial, submergence of self, grace, poise, suppleness, courage, strength and endurance."

Sargent argues that these characteristics are "as valuable to women as to men" and concludes that the dangers of masculinization inherent in athletics are reduced "if the sports are modified for women so as to meet the peculiar qualifications." In other words, athletics for women are fine if adapted to the female body. Athletic competition that pitted men against women, especially playing by men's rules was, therefore, unthinkable, at least to the vast majority of people.

In the 1930s, despite the continued opposition to female competition, there were still opportunities for women to play basketball. So despite the fact that, for example, in 1930 Ohio banned all state tournaments for girls, there were many community organizations providing women's basketball programs. The Dallas Golden Cyclones won the national AAU tournament in 1931 and hired high school student Babe Didrikson by giving her a clerical job that paid $900 a year (adjusted for inflation, about $12,200 today). A year earlier, the Golden Cyclones had been defeated by the Sunoco Oilers in a tournament featuring twenty-eight teams from mostly southern states and held in Kansas. The Midwest was definitely more than open to the notion of women's basketball; some have even described it as a "hotbed" of activity.

In the early 1930s there were also at least two African American female barnstorming teams, out of Philadelphia and Chicago. The Chicago Romas and the Philadelphia Tribunes were big rivals. Interestingly, the star players on each team, Isadore Channels for the Romas and Ora Mae Washington for the Tribunes, had each also won multiple ATA (American Tennis Association) Women's titles.[2]

---

2 Some of this information comes from three excellent books:
Cahn, Susan K. *Coming on Strong: Gender and Sexuality in Twentieth-Century Women's Sport.*
Bearn, Janice A. *From Six-on-Six to Full Court Press: A Century of Iowa Girls' Basketball.*
Lannin, Joanne. *A History of Basketball for Girls and Women: From Bloomers to Big Leagues.*

Back in Cassville, something important was brewing. The details are vague. Some reports suggested that the Olsons hired basketball-playing girls to work in their salons, and the girls themselves formed a team to play against other women. Exactly how it unfolded perhaps is less important than the fact that the Olsons' idea was to field a women's basketball team that represented beauty salons.

The debate about women in sports to this point had been couched in terms of competition or femininity—the prevailing view was that one couldn't have both. So it might've be one thing to have a women's team representing a big, "masculine" energy company, like Sunoco, but a totally different thing to have a team representing a chain of beauty salons. Regardless of the Olsons' intent and how it evolved, the notion of combining athletic competition with beauty was a direct and bold challenge to the cultural view that competition and femininity were mutually exclusive. And the Olsons really threw down the gauntlet when they decided that their team would only play against men using men's rules. If the notion of fielding a basketball team happened organically, at some point there was clear intent on the part of the Olsons to deliberately create a different concept—having women play only against men using men's rules.

The initial local games created a lot of interest and excitement. If they hadn't thought about it before, this ballyhoo must have convinced Ole and Doyle that there was a market for a touring women's team. After all, Ole's Terrible Swedes had been a success, and he had a lot of barnstorming experience on which to draw. By this time the original Swedes had effectively disbanded, although a version of the team continued until the end of the decade. Now, all of Ole's considerable energy and talent could be invested in this new concept. If it was ever just a group of girls who loved to play basketball, it was about to be transformed into a professional team. And this was another leap forward for women—being paid to play sports.

The team needed a coach and a form of transport. Wilbur "Bill" Surface had played with the Swedes, where he was renowned for his outside shooting and described as "a long shot expert." He was still playing occasionally for the Swedes in early 1936. He was also managing the

Olsons' beauty parlors, and soon he switched hairdryers for backboards and became the coach of the Red Heads. Somewhere along the line he met Peggy Lawson, one of the original players and stars of the Red Heads, and later they would become the first of four coach-player couples in Red Heads history.

A photo of that first Red Heads team features not only Surface and Peggy, but also Hazel Vickers Cone, Lera Dunford, Jo and Jean Langerman, and Ruth Osborn. Kay Kirkpatrick Phillips isn't featured in the photo but was on the team. Another member of the team was Leo Hutton, who was the trainer, chaperone, manager, and driver. It wasn't long before Olson had invested in an eight-door station wagon that looked like a very early limo. It cost $3000 and was nicknamed "She Has To," as in she has to have water, she has to have oil, and she has to have gas, according to a story in *PIC Magazine*.

In that *PIC Magazine* feature, the Red Heads are shown playing rummy in a hotel room in Glen Falls, New York, with the observation that rummy was a great game as all seven players could be included. There is also a photo of Kay Kirkpatrick applying makeup with the caption that "glamour can't be neglected—the spectators rank it along with the goals," once again emphasizing the allure of the combination of beauty and competition. And that combination was responsible for a brilliant marketing idea that helped forge the identity of the team.

Lore has it that two members of the original team had red hair, and someone came up with the very, very bright idea that all the team members whose hair wasn't naturally that color should dye it. A 1949 article in the *All Sports News* suggested this version of events:

His [Olson's] first job was to get a name for his team—an unusual moniker if possible. Hundreds of them were considered, but finally Olson's wife, who owned and operated a chain of beauty salons in Missouri and Arkansas suggested "Red Heads." Ole added "All American" to the title and so the name was born. Then he raided the best amateur teams in the land and signed outstanding players.

While it is true that most of the players are natural Red Heads, those who are not don wigs of this hue for their games.

Regardless of how it came about, the Red Heads concept has all the hallmarks of Ole's marketing genius: a visual gimmick that made for great promotional opportunities and helped consolidate the notion that femininity and athletic competition were not mutually exclusive.

The idea of playing solely against men's teams was also a little outlandish. Since the inception of the game, women's basketball had been played with three zones, but that had been recently reduced to two, making women's basketball effectively a two-court game, compared to the men's game. The Red Heads would now have to do something different—run up and down the entire court. Fitness, and the many negative ideas about the suitability of women for athletics, were about to be tested.

Ole and Doyle's intuition proved right. The timing was perfect; the juxtaposition of beauty and athletic competition, the redhead marketing, and the competition against men playing by their rules, were compelling. Crowds showed up in droves to see this unlikely battle of the sexes—as many as a thousand spectators would cram into gyms. And if all this hoopla wasn't enough, Ole incorporated some of the trick plays that endeared the Terrible Swedes to crowds around the country. Then to cap it off, more often than not, the Red Heads would beat their male counterparts. It was a winning package, so much so that before long, Ole had a second team on the road. The Ozark Hillbillies were effectively a farm team for the Red Heads, who were now booked almost every night from fall through the summer. Some of the Hillbillies went on to play for the Red Heads.

It's possible that, initially, the Red Heads played a schedule that was too brutal. An unidentified newspaper article from 1937 reported: "Lately, the Red have been hampered by various injuries of one kind or another— they usually play at least three games per day."

This is supplemented by a report of the previous day's game in Plains, Georgia.

"The All American Red Heads put on a great show here yesterday playing Ellaville's athletic club—they lost 49-21 but the majority of the husky lassies were ailing. Peg Lawson crack forward, was out with minor ailments. Ruth Osburn, big center, who tried to get rough with the Ellavilles, went out with a sprained ankle. Lila Blue had a broken nose, oh 'twas quite sad."

These reports also often referred to the Red Heads' coach as Wiggles Surface, and he was quoted in another article, reflecting on the hectic schedule:

"We average travelling about 135 miles every day, play every night, including Sunday, and on a different court each time. The girls are tired for we just made one of our hardest jumps of the season today. Tomorrow we play in Centerville, S.C.—wherever that is."

At the end of the 1937 season came a report and photo in the *Santa Fe News* announcing the game between the Red Heads and the local St. Michael's Horsemen.

"The purpose of the game is to raise funds for the new Bronson Cutting memorial field. The Horsemen will be at a distinct disadvantage and will probably encounter more difficulty with the rangy feminine quintet than they did against even the champion Albuquerque Bulldogs. Olson's Red Heads will probably have a height advantage of two to three inches per player."

The accompanying photo showed Peggy Lawson, Hazel Vickers, Lera Dunford, Jo and Gene Langerman, and Ruth Osburn standing with their backs to the camera and looking back over their left shoulders.

The Red Heads went from strength to strength. They started getting media coverage wherever they went, and even some places they didn't. They were written about in such famous magazines as *Life* and *Look*. The ambitious Olson had the teams traveling far afield, and in the case of the Red Heads, out of the country. They were actually touring the Philippines on the cusp of American involvement in World War.

The core of the early team consisted of Kay Kirkpatrick, from Waco, Texas, billed as the "Personality Girl."

Hazel Vickers, once described as "the only genuine redhead on the team," was a five-year all-American who played in the Women's World Games in London and was a ball handler and a hotshot. One report said that Hazel "brought the house down with her amazing ability to knock the bottom out of the basket from the middle of the court. She sank six field goals to lead the scoring for the night, and all her shots came from a distance that would baffle all but an All-American girl star."

Peggy Lawson was the chief ball handler and play maker.

Lila Blue, at five feet ten inches, was also a regular.

One addition to the team was already a casualty of war. Torchy Blasch, a Lithuanian, was in Europe when war broke out. She had been working for the Lithuanian government's recreation program, touring the country playing basketball with small-town teams, competing in athletic events, and instructing girls in athletics. She set three Baltic states records, in low hurdles, discus, and shot put. When she came to America her old passport was revoked, leaving her stranded. So she joined the Red Heads and got to see America.

A local paper announced this on April 18, 1940:

C. M. Olson of this city and his nationally known basketball team The All American Red Heads sailed at 4 pm yesterday afternoon, April 17 on the steamer S.S. *Granville* from Los Angeles, Calif., to the Philippine islands to play a schedule of forty games.

Mr. Olson and his famous girls team are due to arrive in Manilla on May 12. They hope to complete their schedule in the Philippines by July 1st.

They left Kansas City over the Santa Fe Chief Monday morning at 9 o'clock. That day a cablegram came here to Mr. Olson from Honolulu, Hawaii asking Mr. Olson to stop there for a series of games on his way to Manila and for another series on the return trip.

The report went on to note that Olson had received the offer to travel to the Far East a few weeks earlier but did not accept until the money offered to him was put in escrow and a "signed contract with a bankable guaranty obtained that all of the expenses of the team and Mr. Olson would be paid for the complete trip above the cash offer for the games."

The report added an interesting side note.

"Mr. Olson had many interesting experiences in making the arrangements for the Philippine trip. Here is one instance: He mailed an air mail letter here Saturday on which the rate was $8.00 The rate is $1 per ounce. His cablegrams cost $1 per word."

The girls actually arrived a day early in Manila. A paper report at the time said, "The Rodriguez brothers who are in charge of the games, received a wire yesterday to the effect that the boat bringing the girls is coming ahead of the stated time."

A printed schedule showed the Red Heads playing an all-Manila girls' team on their opening game in the Philippines and then against a team of all-American men the next night and the Thirty-First Infantry the following day.

CHAPTER 5

1945–1954
The Legend Resumes

● ● ●

*This game was invented to have fun. If you can't
enjoy playing basketball, you've missed a lot.*

—LUTE OLSON

AFTER THE SUCCESSFUL ESCAPE FROM the Philippines, the Red Heads slowed down some from barnstorming. With rationing and other restrictions that came along with World War II, traveling the country playing basketball would be difficult. In addition, as the war progressed, many communities lost their eligible men to the war effort. More and more women were integrated into the economy to help with many different types of endeavors. Some of the Red Heads did end up working in industries that fielded basketball teams, and they played in industrial leagues. But others played with the Red Heads for limited games.

As soon as the war was over, however, Olson had his team on the road once again. In 1945, the Red Heads traveled west. The tall Gene "Careless" Love and Danny Daniels were on that team as the fun resumed. They starred the following year along with Hazel Walker, who was about to take part of a major turning point in Red Heads history.

Hazel Walker was born on August 8, 1914, in Arkansas, the middle child and only daughter of Herbert and Minnie Chancey Walker, both Arkansas natives of part-Cherokee descent.

The athletic Walker played for Ashdown High School as a freshman and was named to all-conference teams three times. In her senior year, Walker and her Pantherettes traveled to Little Rock to compete in Arkansas's first ever girls' state high school basketball tournament. Ashdown lost in the finals, but Walker was named all-state and "Most Beautiful Girl in the Tournament."

According to the *Arkansas Encyclopedia of History and Culture*, Walker was recruited to play for the Tulsa Business College Stenographers. In her second season, she led the Stenos to the 1934 AAU National Championship and was named to her first all-American team.

The Arkansas encyclopedia then goes on to describe what happened next.

After graduating from Tulsa's two-year program, Walker accepted a bookkeeping job with Lion Oil Company in El Dorado (Union County), where she also starred for the company's AAU basketball team, the Oilers. At mid-season, on December 16, 1934, Walker married Everett Eugene (Gene) Crutcher of McGehee (Desha County), a railroad brakeman.

Because married women were not allowed to work at Lion Oil, the couple intended to keep their union a secret until after the national tournament. However, when company chairman T. H. Barton found out, he made an exception to keep his star in an Oilers uniform.

Lion Oil ended sponsorship of its team at the conclusion of the 1936 season, and Walker and her husband moved to Little Rock so she could play for the newly formed Lewis & Norwood Flyers. In five seasons, the Walker-led Flyers lost only eight games on their way to winning national championships in 1937, 1940, and 1941.

Walker continued AAU competition as a player/manager for Arkansas Motor Coaches (1942–1944) and concluded as a player/promoter for Little Rock's Dr. Pepper Girls (1944–1946).

It was then that she signed a professional contract with the Red Heads. Before long, Olson had her as his star player and coach. It seemed like a match made in heaven.

A piece in *All Sports News* at the time reported:

"In Olson's book Hazel Walker is the greatest girl pro player of all time. During 1946–48 Hazel challenged and defeated 97 per cent of all men she contested in a special free throw exhibition. What's more, Hazel does not win in the conventional way of standing erect and tossing 'em in. She kneels then sits flat on the floor—meshing buckets one after the other!"

Another standout from the early post-war era was Gene "Careless" Love, who stood at an imposing six feet four and got her nickname from a popular song of the time. Other Red Heads regulars were Peaches Hatcher, Margie Arends, Betty Arends, and "Stubby" Winter, who was almost a foot shorter than Love.

In 1948, Olson approached an English teacher by the name of Orwell Moore to become coach of the Red Heads' second team, the Famous Red Heads. Moore was not just a teacher; he was an avid basketball fan and coach. He also coached baseball, which might have originally been his first love. He had a dream to play for the St. Louis Cardinals, but his impact on the sporting world was to take a different and arguably greater turn. Orwell was also a Boy Scout leader. Olson probably saw in Moore some of his own off-court qualities: great business acumen and marketing intelligence. On the court, Moore shared Olson's creativity and innovation. The only reason Olson did not make Moore the coach of the All-American Red Heads was that he had already appointed Hazel Walker as the first female Red Heads coach.

Moore, being a tough businessman in his own right, had some conditions he needed to have met before taking the job. One of those conditions turned out to be a huge plus for the Red Heads for the next decade and beyond. Moore insisted that his wife, Lorene, also known as "Butch," an enthusiastic and excellent player in her own right, be allowed to join the team. Olson agreed and thus two legends were born. Butch went on to have an incredible career with the Red Heads, scoring more than thirty-five thousand points. Orwell became an iconic head coach and within a few years found himself the owner of the Red Heads dynasty.

However, none of this had seemed likely just a few short years before. Then, as a young man, Orwell, who had already been smitten with Lorene "Butch," started coughing up blood, and he knew what that meant—the return of his tuberculosis. He said a sad good-bye to Lorene and headed for the sanitarium. Orwell and Lorene exchanged many letters, but he discouraged her from visiting him because the sanitarium was, in his mind, a sick and deathly place. In fact, he told Lorene to forget about marriage. He thought he was going to die. In addition, Moore had some concerns about the age difference between him and Lorene. He was twenty-six, and she was just sixteen. Marriages of that nature were not uncommon at that time, but Orwell was still concerned about the age gap.

In an interview later in his career, Moore recalled the turning point.

"One night after dinner, I was talking to the guy across the hall. He said his latest X-ray had come back negative and he was going home to raise chickens. That was all he wanted. Everyone there wanted just a little bit more of life, a little bit of love. The next morning, he had passed away."

Moore called Lorene the next day, and they were soon married. He recovered fully the next spring and returned home to his native Caraway, Arkansas, to become coach and athletic director of Caraway High School.

Although Moore started out as coach for the Famous Red Heads, who toured the western half of the United States, it was not long before he was promoted to coach the main event. Orwell Moore arguably had more business, marketing, and coaching experience than Hazel Walker, so perhaps it would have only been a matter of time before he replaced her as the All American Red Heads coach. However, that process was sped along when Olson discovered that Hazel Walker was exploring the idea of launching her own women's team. That discovery went down with Olson as well as an opponent's shot. Walker was out and Orwell Moore elevated to coach the All American Red Heads.

Hazel Walker did indeed field her own team. Her Arkansas Travelers also barnstormed the country until 1965. Hazel died in 1990 and was inducted into the Arkansas Sports Hall of Fame and, in 2001, the Women's Basketball Hall of Fame.

Coach Moore was ahead of his time in many ways. He constantly was writing down notes about plays, professionalism, the mental aspect of the game, and what he wanted from his players. His notes are part John Wooden and part Tony Robbins.

Here is a list of some things he wanted from his players that he wrote down while staying at the Hotel Denny in Madison, Indiana. The list is exactly what any coach or leader would write today, some seventy years later.

I want my players to love me not hate me.
I want my players to respect me not to fear me.
I want my players to have faith in me not to distrust me.
I want my players to be with me not against me.
I want my players to carry out my assignments with a special thrill and to do the assignment with zest and enthusiasm for the privilege of carrying out a special job.
I want my players to be ball players not just a group.
I want my players to be quick at taking instruction.
I want my players to remember that they are professional job holders not a group of amateurs whose behavior is dictated by moods, whims, likes and dislikes.
I want my players to be able to take criticism and make the most of it.
I want my players to be able to change on my advice.
I want my players to be my kind of players.

And if that wasn't clear enough, Moore had three other general principles.

Call me Coach, not Mr. Moore.
I want your attention.
Listen and Do!

Within a couple of years, Coach Moore had a dynamic team. A newspaper report of the 1950 team points out that in 1948 the Red Heads scored an all-time high seventy-four points (no three-pointers in those days). However, the article claimed that the girls' aim was to entertain rather than win.

"Their main ambition is to give the fans a really good time, and a helluva show. They invariably succeed, sometimes under the most trying circumstances. "

Coach Moore explained this philosophy.

"In one season my girls will play around 180 games. The season is about six months—November to May. If these kids were to go full steam every night they couldn't stand up under the schedule. We'll always play hard and give the paying people a show, but we don't aim to win 'em all— and we don't try."

The unidentified newspaper gives a glimpse of what the girls faced when traveling:

"An avalanche of publicity precedes the far-roving Reds wherever they go and wherever they play. Coach Moore doubles as a chauffeur for the team and the girls are easily recognizable as they zoom along the highways in Ole Olson's DeSoto. Gas station attendants, love the kids, policemen wave their legal greetings, male pedestrians emit prosaic wolf-whistles."

The article also focused on a new Red Head, "Red" Mason:

Olson, Moore and a good portion of the fans who came out to see the Red Heads share the feeling that 140-pound Mason of Siloam Springs, Arkansas, is the bona fide queen of the 1950 quintet. Not that effervescent Red resembles Betty Grable when she's in her working clothes because she doesn't. But she has personality and a little chipped tooth in the front of her mouth, and an odd way of inspiring mirth from audiences that might otherwise sit on their hands.

Like the other Red Heads, Miss Mason is a farmerette, but she is probably the top technician in her field of femme basketball comediennes. Red is to girls' basketball what Betty Hutton is to light cinema comedy. She provokes a laugh when a game may begin to develop the earmarks of a soporific. In addition, she's a competent set-shot, an expert passer, a wizard at ball-dribbling between her legs, and trucking with the ball spinning on her finger tips.

A piece in the *All-Sports News* reveals some other details about Red Mason.

"Recently, Ole Olson has come up with a young gal named Red Mason, who is actually a redhead and boasts enough theatrical and dramatic ability to make good on the screen. As a matter of fact, she is being considered for a part in the movies, for she is exceptional in staging a comedy act in basketball such has never been seen."

If Red Mason was the queen of entertainment, then Lorene "Butch" Moore was the princess of scoring. Despite Coach Moore's stated goal of not trying to win every game, in 1950 the Red Heads won 129 out of 169 games played and surpassed that in 1953, winning 134 games. In many of those games, Lorene "Butch" Moore was top scorer.

In 1950 Ole Olson obtained a copyright for the All American Red Heads in the categories of sports, athletic amusement, and entertainment.

One aspect of the Red Heads was their indefatigability. In an era when the car was relatively new, the notion of traveling forty thousand miles in a few months seemed ridiculous, especially when after a long day's travel, the girls took to the court to challenge the men in many different venues. In the 1950s they played in front of fifteen thousand people in Chicago one night and then five hundred in a small community the next.

The Nampa High School (Idaho) paper, the *Nampa Growl*, reported a 1951 game against an Austin junior college team.

"The gals could play basketball and showed excellent form whipping the ball around and shooting. Top honors went to Butch Moore, only 5'6" but she went to work in the slot with a vengeance and her swing shots netted 22 points."

Red Mason was the next-highest scorer and only other Red Head in double figures with twelve.

"Red Mason put on the best show. She strolled down court with the ball spinning on her finger, dribbled the ball between her legs and late in the game decided to do some officiating when referee Lindgren couldn't take the pace."

After the game Coach Moore said poetically, "Seven heavenly bodies beat 11 shooting stars tonight."

The final score was 57–48. Thirteen hundred people watched the game, which raised $293 for the purchase of new uniforms for the high school's baseball team.

In another game that year, the Red Heads defeated a team of former college all-stars 72–71. Typically, Moore was top scorer and Mason top entertainer.

Butch canned 16 fielders during the game, most of them from well out on the floor. Her 32 points led all scoring.

Sharing the spotlight with Butch was Red Mason, a little (5 feet 8 inches that is an Arkansas hillbilly with a flair for comedy and a generous supply of high speed energy. Between her numerous gags, Red managed to hit 16 points.

It went on night after night and occasionally night after day in a doubleheader. In a game in Springfield, Missouri, the Red Heads defeated Stag Collegians 58–48, with Moore top scoring with 20 points and Mason 16.

Wherever they went the Red Heads earned admiration and respect, and not just for their athletic skills. Here is a piece from the county record from Denton, Maryland, that almost certainly represented the views of the majority of people who saw the Red Heads play.

A wonderful bunch of girls. That is about the only way you can express your feelings that you have when you talk to these girls. For a bunch of young ladies who are traveling every day and night of the year and are up to competitive spirit each and every night. These young ladies moved into our town early Friday afternoon after just completing 10 games in 8 days. Then at 8:30 pm Friday night, they moved out on the floor of our armory and put across one of the best and certainly the funniest basketball games that I have ever witnessed. A crowd of 486 people squeezed into the armory and watched these girls do everything from rubbing bald heads to knocking down our largest player. Trick shots, good shots and a truly competitive spirit that you will have to go far to match.

The men's team that participated for Denton should feel lucky to play against such ladies as this. Good looking and a head of red hair that if we did not know better should betray a wild and wooly temper. But the hair only seemed to affect the funny bone. From Choctaw Indians (which one of them was) to the nicest girls (which they all were) we owe a vote of thanks for the note of levity that was instilled into us by their visit. And we hope that the Denton Athletic Association brings them back and not in the too distant future.

The comedy and trick shots were always on show along with athletic talent and class. During this post-war period, Red Mason typically led the comedic routines, often before the tip-off. One paper account described the powder-puff act, in which Mason "accosted referee Spike Liebbe with a giant economy size powder puff just before the whistle."

Later, Mason switched position with the referees, and her officiating left a lot to be desired! In a typical act, Mason donned cane, top hat, and a huge pair of glasses and called a foul every time the opposition got the ball, with calls such as, "You're walking with the ball." The points scored during these antics generally were not recorded and didn't feature in the final score.

Butch Moore always entertained with her overhead shot from the free-throw line and her piggy-back shot with Myrtle Wallace, in which the ball was "whipped over the top of the defense to Moore riding on Wallace's shoulders and Butch plunked it in from there."

Moore and Mason both, of course, did under-the-legs dribbling, often going under teammates and opponents. The baseball stunt was also popular, with the girls forming a diamond, the "pitcher" delivering the ball to the hitter, and the ball somehow ending up in the basket.

Sometimes it was Moore who led the ribbing of the refs. One report of a game told how Moore donned top hat, cane, and glasses and then exchanged places with referee Red Nickell. When Nickell, playing in Moore's place, was fouled and missed a free throw, "he received a boot in the pants from Butch and was moved up to within five feet of the basket for the next free throw."

The Red Heads were truly loved. Here's a piece from a Winnipeg newspaper about a 1953 visit: "The Red Heads slayed the clients with two full hours of belly laughs and raised the stout auditorium roof several inches when someone suggested a return engagement. It can't happen too soon."

In another report from the post-war era, one writer introduced his article on the Red Heads like this:

Please quote me on this. And chalk up an assist for Amram Scheinfeld, an erudite gentleman who writes with authority on the problems of heredity and the sexes.

Women are tougher than men. They are more rugged. They can take more punishment. After it all, they are apt to live longer. My chief source is Mr. Scheinfeld. But I have done further research on the problem. I have seen Ole Olson's original All-American Red Heads play basketball.

Admission fees to games during this era were anything from fifty cents to two dollars and fifty cents, and some of the proceeds of the games went to pay for either school or civic activities, mostly athletics related, like high school uniforms or improvements to ballparks and other sporting facilities. However, some games against civic organizations raised funds for other causes. In one game played in Denver and organized by the Elks, some proceeds went toward the operation of a children's home. Incidentally, the girls won the game 52–50, mainly on the back of Butch Moore, "who was good for six straight 40-footer buckets, to put the Red Heads back in the game when they were trailing by ten points."

Two regulars of the early fifties were Bonnie Gilliland and Ruby Hayes, both six footers, and the athletic Myrtle Wallace, who featured in that piggy-back routine. Johnny Farley was a clever playmaker who made a formidable backcourt with Red Mason.

During this era the Red Heads were featured in countless papers and *Basketball Illustrated, PIC* (Philippines), *Colliers, Basketball National, Clair Bee's Annual Sportsvue, Sporting News, Sport Life, Southern Coach and Athlete,* and many others. However, their exposure was about to explode. Moreover, there was about to be a critical change in the Red Heads organization.

CHAPTER 6

1955–1960
The Legend Expands

● ● ●

The old saying "I'm doing my best" is not near good enough.
By what standards are you judging your best? How do you
know it's your best? What are your expectations? What are
your objectives? What are your values? Doing your best is not
enough. You must perform with efficiency and proficiency. You
must pay the price to win and perform like a champion.

—ORWELL MOORE

By 1954, THE RED HEADS were a national phenomenon. They were drawing crowds and media attention, being featured in newspapers, magazines, and on the increasingly available television. Coach Orwell Moore, helped considerably by one of his star players, wife Lorene, had taken the Red Heads to new heights.

Olson's Red Heads had been in existence for almost twenty years, although there was the break for World War II. Moore had followed Olson's tradition and philosophy and developed a team and a concept for the times. It is no surprise, therefore, when Ole decided it was time to step away from the game and the ownership of the team, that he chose Moore as the natural successor. In 1954 Moore acquired the Red Heads from Olson.

In a later interview, Moore said that Olson wanted to sell the team to him. "He thought I would take care of them. When he first approached me, I said, 'I can't pay the interest on this.'"

Olson apparently said, "There won't be any interest." Moore later said, "It took me ten years to pay for 'em."

In the last chapter, we saw Orwell Moore's no-nonsense approach to coaching and playing the game. Now that he was the owner of the team, he could be very explicit about what he wanted from his players both on and off the court.

Moore wrote down on notebook paper

RULES FOR RED HEADS: BE A GOOD RED HEAD

1. There will be no sleeping in car: just prior to a game if we are late arriving.
2. Never just wake up and go into gas station or restaurant without refreshing a bit, and most of all comb hair. Always be presentable or do not leave the car. Remember: You are always on display.
3. There will be no joke telling in the car. No vulgar language or black gardening. To be a good Red Head you must think clean, be clean and live clean.
4. Never sit in a hotel lobby or restaurant and read mail. Always wait until you get to your room out of public view. Do not go asking clerk for mail. I will get it and hand it out.
5. No one girl is to ever go out alone. There will always be at least two of you.
6. You are never to travel with hair curled.
7. Never smoke in the town you are playing in, in public.
8. Always straighten up room in motel or hotel before leaving in the morning
9. Every girl loads and unloads her own luggage.
10. Always be nice to people, especially those who are responsible for us being there.

The rules give some insight into what it was like to be a Red Head during this era. There was a lot of time spent in the car and in public. There were high expectations of the girls, and they had to be "on" all the time. This was part of their brand as well as good marketing and promotion.

Today, when we can call almost anyone on the planet at any time, it is hard to conceive of or even remember a time when mail was the main—and often only—form of communication. Being on the road as a member of the Red Heads was glamorous, but it was not easy. One can only imagine how homesick some of the girls were after weeks and weeks on the road without a day off. So news from the world beyond the Red Heads bubble—news from family and from home—would always be very welcome. Hence Moore's Fourth Commandment.

Another fact that might seem surprising, looking back sixty years, is that it is apparent that some of the girls smoked. It is almost inconceivable that a professional athlete today, given a similarly brutal schedule as the Red Heads', would even think of smoking. It was at precisely this time that Dr. Richard Doll in England was publishing research suggesting that smoking could be harmful to health, but such research had not yet penetrated the public consciousness. In 1954 a famous study, the British doctors' study, which looked at the health of forty thousand doctors over two decades, concluded that smoking was indeed harmful to health, which prompted the United Kingdom's government to warn for the first time that smoking and lung cancer were related.

Coach Moore was not just trying to protect the reputation—and brand—of the Red Heads; like every great coach, he was also trying to mentor his players in life as well as basketball. He knew that how one conducted oneself off the court had a direct relationship to one's play on the court. The Red Heads were not just being coached in basketball.

Moore himself looked to his own background for inspiration. His father taught him about hard work, self-reliance, and morality. His mother taught him about sacrifice, love, and faith. Moral values were his foundation and his heritage. It's no surprise that he emphasized these qualities when coaching and mentoring.

In a handwritten note entitled "Who Are You?" Moore put into perspective what he thought was important about being a Red Head.

A Red Head is a special person with a wonderful purpose and a message to all;
'Come let me lift you up' to be a better person, a better family, a better nation; come visit with me, come and see right, purposeful living and championship performance. Emit a radiance that will reflect a glow in the hearts of people from every station of life.

One can almost imagine Coach Moore speaking these next words, not just to the Red Heads players but also in schools and colleges, to young adults and even not-so-young adults. He did speak a lot at schools and colleges, encouraging young women not just to excel in athletics, but also to be wholehearted in their pursuit of excellence in life.

Here's an excerpt from one of his talks:

"'Just who are you?' Do you have an identity other than a social security number? Do you have a purpose? Do you have any objectives of achievement? Do you have any personal standards of conduct? Can you think? Do you study? Do you plan? Or are you just drifting along in the stream of society aimlessly, without a purpose, without a goal, without the armor of moral ethics, without God?"

With these guiding principles, great business acumen, and insight into how to elicit peak performance, Moore was about to take the Red Heads to new heights. Coach Moore believed that peak athletic performance had more to do with the mind than the body, a concept that was not as accepted then as it is today. Here are some of his thoughts, fortunately still preserved on the original notepaper, about the importance of mental skills:

"For every physical skill there is a mental skill that goes with it."

What we know from recent neuroscience research is that while there is indeed a motor skill programmed into the brain through practice, there is also a set of psychological factors—for example, mood, anxiety, and even timing—that influence the performance of that skill.

"Basketball players are made, not born."

"Most fears in athletes are very unreal. What you fear is not there."

This is true. Again, recent research in thought processes and cognitive bias has shown that we overestimate and exaggerate our fears.

"More players fail mentally than physically."

"Success is a frame of mind."

"You must like to see your teammates succeed."

"One girl's glory must be the other girl's success."

"Look at your teammates and your coach through your heart and not your eyes—there is a difference."

"90% of your performance depends on the proper mental attitude."

"All athletes make mistakes; smart athletes make fewer mistakes."

"The secret of memory is interest."

This is also very true. We now indeed know that emotion is important in memory, because it determines focus and attention, among other things.

"Enthusiasm and interest are keys to success."

"You must be mentally tough to be a champion."

"Success is a journey."

"You must pay the price to be a winner. You must pay the price in your individual work and teamwork and you must pay the price in your game performance. You must be willing and able to pay the price if you want to be a winner."

"Athletes learn every day that there is no fairness in life, so do not demand it."

"Play inspired and I will see you at the top."

In 1955, the first season under new ownership, Moore moved the team to his hometown of Caraway, Arkansas. The town had one of the largest school districts in the area and a decent economy, and it would be the home to the Red Heads for the rest of their existence.

In 1956, the Red Heads visited Alaska for the first time. It was to be one of four visits made to the northern outpost. For the girls who made the trip, it was an adventure that they surely wouldn't have made if they had not been representing the best women's basketball team in the world. The girls who made the trip were Red Mason, Butch Moore, Jesse Banks,

Zethal Keith, Kathryn Pitcock, Sammy Autry, and Shelvia "Shorty" Johnson, who was, of course, six feet five inches tall.

The Red Heads were entertained by the natives, from Ketchikan to Fairbanks, from Juneau to Anchorage. They were invited to dance with elders, play with Eskimo children, and play against the guys at various military installations. Later, the players recall getting letters from the Eskimo children they had so impressed.

In some places there was concern that if there was a whale sighting, there might not be many people in attendance at the Red Heads games. Fortunately, there were no whales, and the only sights were of the Red Heads performing their entertaining magic on the floor. However, the men's teams were not very hospitable, winning as many games as they lost during the Red Heads sixteen-game tour. The weather conditions were generally favorable to travel even though it was fall, but the team was fogged in at Point Barrow (also known as Nuvuk) on the arctic coast—the northernmost part of the United States at less than thirteen hundred nautical miles from the North Pole.

The *Anchorage Daily News* of October 25, 1956, reported on the last leg of the tour: "The All American Red Heads fell to the charms of the Anchorage Basketball League All Stars 48–46 last night but not before more than a one thousand fans saw one of the funniest sports shows since the Globetrotters were here several years ago."

Moore and Mason scored thirty of the Red Heads' points but fell short when a shot hit the rim as time expired.

The following night the two most famous Red Heads were at it again. This time the *Anchorage Daily Times* reported this: "Again last night Red Mason and Butch Moore paced the visitors. The former combining her hook shot with some long range shots, paced all players with 26 points. But it was Butch Moore's shooting that won the admiration of the crowd. She scored 24 points all but one basket coming from far out."

Tribute from teammate Jesse Banks
Professor Emeritus
University of Southern Colorado

I think Lorene "Butch" Moore was one of the most fundamentally gifted players that I played with. She knew the game tremendously, her shooting was outstanding, and her ball handling was just unbelievable.

Another player whom I still look upon as the greatest was Willa Fay Red Mason. I don't know that I've ever seen anyone since that could do the things she could do. She kept the crowd laughing. I think I laughed when she did something funny every night. Remember if you are playing with somebody for over two hundred games, you've seen it all, but she was always doing something that was outstanding.

Alaska was memorable in many ways. For example, Sammye Autrey was called in at the last minute to replace the sick Butch Moore. Sammye received a marriage proposal. (Men vastly outnumbered women in Alaska at that time.) On another occasion, the Red Heads were flying in a seaplane when one of the two engines went out. The pilot decided it would be smart idea to return rather than continue. They had just landed when the other engine failed!

Jackie Wragg Remembers Alaska

In Ketchikan we walked to a totem park that was so interesting and also toured a tuberculosis hospital for Native American Eskimos.

In Sitka, we landed by seaplane, and when we disembarked onto the dock there was an open boat with a huge moose head in it.

In Fairbanks we visited a museum, and there was an enormous bear at the entrance.

In Anchorage the game sponsors met us at the airport and then paraded us up the main street. They had Red Heads posters all over their cars.

The trip to Alaska proved so successful that the Red Heads returned the following year. By then they were a national sensation. They had appeared on the hit show *What's My Line?* and a variation, *I've Got a Secret*, hosted by Gary Moore. They also appeared on the *Ed Sullivan Show*, which was a popular Sunday-night show that aired from New York. The girls traveled in casual clothes and had to call home to get something special to wear. Jackie Wragge recalled, "I had my three-inch heels and a wool-knit suit dress sent."

The other guests were singer Roberta Sherwood, the DeMarco sisters, a performing dog act, and Red Buttons. Jackie recalled, "We were slated to be the last several minutes of the show, which made us a bit nervous. But nothing compared to Red Buttons! He completely mangled a wire hanger as he paced back and forth backstage in front of us."

Apart from national shows, the girls were getting all sorts of other media attention.

For example, the *Silver Dollar Gazette* out of Silver Dollar City, Branson, Missouri, ran an interesting story about the Red Heads in this era. The motto of the paper was, "We print the truth and all other news." At least they were honest! Their headline read as follows:

ALL AMERICAN RED HEADS OF CARAWAY, ARKANSAS

Held in silver dollar city jail for disturbing Peace: Sheriff expected to recover

The games went on against all types of opposition. In a game played in the Pueblo Catholic High School Gym, the Red Heads played against the ominously named Jones Mortuary. Fans were dying to get in to the game. It was a grave encounter but the Red Heads executed well and buried the Mortuary Men 59–52. Butch Moore was killing it from the outside as usual and finished as high scorer with 25.

I am sure this piece made a great publicity stunt!

Tribute from Shirley "Trooper" Howard

My experience with the Red Heads was wonderful; I especially remember the Alaska tour and being on the *Ed Sullivan Show*.

I always had two idols with the Red Heads. They were Butch Moore and Red Mason. I always wanted to be as good as they were. I tried, but no one could fill their shoes.

By the late fifties the two main stars of the era, Red Mason and Butch Moore, had retired from playing. They were both instrumental in raising the level of play and entertainment of the Red Heads. Moore, who played for eleven seasons including time with the Famous Red Heads, racked up 35,426 points. Mason played for ten seasons. Others who were no longer with the team by the time the fifties came to an end were the tall Zethel Keith from Louisiana and the even taller "Shorty" Johnson. Kathryn Pitcock from Tennessee also retired.

Lorene "Butch" Moore Remembers

We were playing in a little timber mining town in Oregon. We played a very good game and won, and afterward the players and their wives came to where we were having dinner and talked and entertained us. The next day the guy who had organized the event called Orwell and said he wanted to see him. Orwell went and got a big surprise. The man had their share of the gate money and gave it to Orwell and told him to share it among the girls. I think it was about $300. He said, "Now you give it to the six girls, because we want them to have it." Boy, we were we excited about that!

We never forgot that town, and we always wanted to go back there and play, and we did—but we never got a deal like that again.

It wasn't just the players who were changing as the swinging sixties rolled around. As Orwell Moore wanted to spend more time on the business side, he turned the coaching duties over to Glynn Greene for the 1959 and 1960 seasons, but in 1961 a new coach was hired.

Lorene "Butch" Moore Remembers

Another thing that made our team outstanding was that we had a warm feeling for each other. Fellowship on the team was paramount. We felt and cared for each other. If one person got hurt, we were right there. When some guys decided to show off on the court or even manhandle a girl, he soon felt the wrath of the whole Red Heads team—and the crowd.

Basketball was more than a game. In a great performance, you would find yourself soaring above the crowd. It was an emotional high. This was a place that not everyone can reach. It was far more than just winning a basketball game. It was something that gave us a sense of being.

Another game I remember was playing in Sioux City, Iowa. Ole had closed out the eastern unit and called on us to play the last of their games. We knew we were going to have a great crowd; it was standing room only. We were at our best that night and played one of our greatest games. We lost by six points.

By the time he retired as a coach, Orwell Moore had not only inspired his team and built an international phenomenon, but he had also taken the Red Heads to new heights both as athletes and as entertainers. Specifically, he had built on Ole Olson's platform and introduced a new half-time show that was worth the price of admission on its own. The show included dazzling ball handling, juggling, passing, and shooting from improbable positions. It also included a variety of original basketball gags, like the la conga out-of-bounds play, the boy in the balcony shot, and the mule train out-of-bounds play.

Moore introduced knee dribbling for the first time. He drew up the plays on pieces of paper, some of which, fortunately, have been preserved. Moore was meticulous in his instructions about each player's role in the execution of the play. These gags were practiced repeatedly until the girls could perform them in their sleep—while smiling.

But now Orwell decided to turn the coaching duties over to someone else, and in 1960 he chose Ben Overman. Ben Overman had known the Moores for a long time and had actually helped them with some of the Red Heads marketing chores. He too was a native of Caraway, a lover of basketball, and a great choice to lead the Red Heads into another era.

Lorene "Butch" Moore Remembers

Playing in Winnipeg was a thrill. The Red Heads had never played there before. We got there, and we were warmly greeted by the Canadian people and the press, and several men and their wives came to visit us. We were playing the men's AAU Canadian champions. So we went out there and worked hard that night, and the Canadians loved us. I scored thirty-two points and was so proud of us. We played a heck of game and ended up losing by two points.

The last two games I played I had a family; Tammy and Burnie were both little. We had a young man run our third-unit team; he was a fine man, and we liked him very much. One of our big girls got hurt, and we didn't have anyone to put in her place. So Orwell encouraged me to go in. This was in our home territory—Cloverben, Arkansas, about fifty miles from Caraway—and we knew we were going to have a large crowd. Orwell told me not to worry about scoring; I could entertain people without even making a basket. Well, I had a great night; I scored thirty-seven points. Even though I was an old lady with two children, I was so excited about playing basketball again. The next night it was the same thing. I was so sore from the night before, however, so I only scored six points in my last game as a Red Head.

CHAPTER 7

A Day on the Road

Orwell Moore

● ● ●

Part of the richness of your relationship is the ability
to see through the eyes of your teammates.

—ORWELL MOORE

WHEN TRAVELING WITH THE ALL American Red Heads, I would get up in the morning and check the weather forecast. Weather was a very important factor in travel plans. Next, I would review the schedule to determine how many miles we needed in order to arrive in time for the next game.

Players all got up, had breakfast, and cleaned up their rooms. It was very important that they leave their hotel or motel rooms in order. The coach inspected the rooms. We didn't want the motel and hotel people to say we couldn't stay with them anymore. We did not want to leave anything broken, torn up, or in disarray. If the girls happened to break a lamp or destroy something, they reported that to me. I in turn reported it to the hotel manager the morning before leaving. If there was a cost, I would pay them; we didn't like exaggerating the cost after we left. It was good business for us to do things that way.

My morning rule (Moore Rule) was that everybody, when seeing each other, would say hello. In a hearty and brisk way, "Good morning!" was spoken to everybody. That was a rule that would stand throughout my tenure as a coach with the All American Red Heads and as the owner.

We loaded our own luggage and equipment. As far as seating arrangements, the girls rotated seats; there were several reasons for that. Number one, it was colder in the backseat than it was in the middle and front seats, so each girl, including Lorene, followed the same rotation rules. The girls who sat in the front seat were responsible for reading the map, making sure that we made the correct turns, as well as looking for places that we could visit. Stopping and visiting many national sights, parks, and attractions was very important to the teams. Let me give another example of how we did a day on the road.

When going to Colorado Springs, we often visited the Gardens of the Gods, and we might have a picnic with plenty of food and a lot of fun. We enjoyed the scenery in the Gardens of the Gods. A day with the Red Heads might include meeting a senator, a governor, or other significant people. We played at many Indian reservations. The All American Red Heads loved the adventure, and being on the road created a lot of this.

When they wrote home, I wanted my girls to say that we saw the Garden of the Gods or the Painted Desert or the Navajo Indian reservations. This was always a part of our travels, to look for national sights the girls could carry home as a part of their educations. I still remember the places I visited, like the Grand Canyon and several caves, but there are too many places to list. That was just part of our day.

If it was a bright and nice day there was always roadwork. Athletes know it's very important. Roadwork helped us keep in good physical condition; we had to be in good condition to play our games. Roadwork was usually three quarters of a mile; sometimes we would extend it to a mile, enough to get the blood flowing well. It was understood that the girls did this in a group for safety; nobody would fall behind. A lot of the time there were dogs along the road or near houses, which made things interesting, although we were on the main road. A girl was never left behind the group. Workouts consisted of a brisk walk and then about a fifty-yard run called a wind sprint. That type of running helps with the burst of energy needed to play the games.

On rainy and bad weather days, we practiced jump-ball situations someplace where they were not in the bad weather. Men thinking the girls couldn't jump got a surprise; we learned to get up there. Girls didn't normally jump very well back in those days; we did have some girls who could jump. They could soar—they could get up there. Another advantage our girls had was the technique of not striking the ball on the side; they went for the underside of the ball, which gave them another four-inch advantage. Most of the guys tapped the ball on the side. Sometimes we could gain control of the ball by our quickness, getting out there and hitting underneath the ball. Possession of the ball is the most important factor in basketball games. You've got to have possession of the basketball.

We would practice for the half-time show by juggling, working on ball-handling routines, and spinning, and then we would work on pivoting. We were strong on pivoting. That's one of the greatest things that basketball players can learn is how to pivot—forward, backward, and the back step.

Maybe some of my girls were not happy with their performances during the half-time show. Often, I would get up and look out the door after a game; if it was warm they would be outside practicing. I'd say that every girl who played for us went to sleep with a basketball in her bed. That was something that she lived by; she knew she had to perform. She went about it in the most devoted manner. I'm very proud of the girls who did that; they wanted to show what they could do with a basketball. That was a challenge that worked for everyone.

We went to juggling shows. We saw a guy in Las Vegas. He came down and talked with us for about two hours the morning after his show, helping us with juggling. Some of the things he could do we never learned, because he was very skillful. The most important thing that he told us was that an object like a basketball couldn't move as fast as an individual—that a person was twice as fast. We learned that we could snatch the ball when it was falling, helping in our routines.

It was a daily routine to check the schedule where we were playing the next day. Sometimes we knew in advance that we had TV and radio interviews or personal appearances. Some of the radio interview questions were unusual, but our kids handled that very well. In fact, we practiced doing interviews on the road, being sure to be positive about what we said about the Red Heads. The girls learned to be skillful doing interviews. We practiced each day, talking about interviews with newspaper and magazine writers; sometimes I would be the person asking the questions, but a lot of times it would be Red Mason, Johnny Farley, Butch Moore, or one of the other girls asking the questions.

After arriving in town, I would call the person in charge, letting him know that we were in town, checking to see if he had anything planned for us. I checked on the advanced ticket sales, which was one of my jobs, and saw how we were going to handle them that night and the gate receipts. The players dressed in uniforms and warm-ups before leaving for the gymnasium. Many of the old gyms didn't provide very good dressing-room facilities. We took care of that; our warm-ups were made of good heavy material, always with a zippered hood. We always went to the game together—that was a rule. It didn't make a difference if parents were visiting; the players all rode to the game as a team.

Parents and friends would often come to the games. It was a rule that while warming up, the girls could wave to parents or friends to let them know they were seen. They were, however, not to go up and sit with their relatives, which was the rule. They needed to remember that this was their job, and they were getting paid to play. After the game was the time for visiting.

In the beginning, Olson did the scheduling for all the games; he sent us the dates, the terms, the towns we were playing in, the lodging, the reservations that had been made. If there were no motels or hotels in that town, we stayed in a town nearby. Before receiving the new schedule everybody was eager to know where we were going to play. Were we heading west or were we heading east? After receiving the schedule, we called a jam session to discuss it. The schedule was not to be given to anyone other than parents. Mr. Olson found out with experience that some organizations would also schedule an event in the town, causing a conflict. The player mailed the schedule to the players' moms and dads; some would put it on their refrigerators and track the towns with circles. The neighbors would visit wanting to know where the team would be playing.

When the relatives came to visit, the mother could go into the room, but no males were allowed in the rooms that belonged to the Red Heads. That rule was ironclad. So the schedule came, and we saw a doubleheader on this date. My girls wanted to set records; they wanted to win more games than the previous teams. We had to play more games to break the records. They didn't gripe about playing a doubleheader on Saturday or Sunday afternoons. At the bottom of the schedule, Mr. Olson would write, "Dinner on me after each doubleheader." During holidays, dinner was funded by Mr. Olson—the finest restaurants on Thanksgiving and Christmas. The whole team had to attend the dinners. That was fellowship time that we had on the road. Those were some of the important things that we did on the road; we observed the rules and regulations of living together. Our girls were strong; we never got down on our hands and knees, and for that reason we were lucky not to come up with a lot of injuries. I didn't even have a first-aid kit with me. We had some sprained ankles, contused thumbs, maybe a bumped nose. One time Jolene Ammons got her nose broken, which was one of the most serious accidents. It was the coach's job to look after the medical situations.

After each game we went to eat. Of course, there were always people talking with the Red Heads. The girls were signing autographs while being asked where they would be playing tomorrow. There was always good rapport. After a lot of Saturday-night games, we didn't have to get up early, so we could sleep late. On many Sunday mornings, the girls wanted to go to church; these kids were church-going people. They had been raised in the community to be leaders and believe in God. Some of the girls would call the church of their choice saying they were from the All-American Red Heads and would like to attend church. In our travels we did not wear dresses, only slacks, but never in the history of the Red Heads were they turned down due to attire. They always made it to church on their own, because often I was busy or trying to catch up on much-needed sleep. At church they were well received. The minster would recognize them, asking them to stand up. After service a lot of the folks would invite the girls for Sunday dinner, but of course, the girls could not accept the invitations—we were headed out of town for another game.

CHAPTER 8

Who Are the Red Heads?

Orwell Moore

● ● ●

Class is more important than a game.

—PAT SUMMITT

I'VE BEEN ASKED MANY TIMES by people who wanted to promote the games for the All American Red Heads, by booking agencies, by curiosity seekers, and by fans who came to see the game and who loved the game—what is it like to travel with the All American Red Heads? What are they like? What are their special activities? Do the girls have any special rules that you travel by? Of course I tried to answer questions the best that I could with the time that I had. I will describe the All American Red Heads basketball teams.

They were in super good health. They had positive attitudes and explosive personalities. They had a great urge to learn. Everyone had a great passion for playing basketball. They had the desire to be professionals and were determined to be a on a professional level. They were able to follow a game plan with fundamentals and techniques. Teamwork was what made the girls strong performers. Attitude was the magic factor and a sign of good things to come. They presented professional polish, court presence, and flair. A Red Head was able to walk the walk and talk the talk, which was the true part of the Red Heads. It wasn't the stuff they had going that made them great. The stuff that they added to the things they had going for them was what made them great.

The real Red Heads were like a family—each team like a family unit, sharing, caring, and looking at their teammates through their hearts and not through their eyes. Each girl realized that to be an All American Red Head, you had to become a special person. The All-American Red Heads were special people. They were inspired by the flame of crowds' approval and the great pride of the All American Red Heads, which we call the Crimson Pride. The Red Heads climbed the ladder of achievement and gained the heights of professionalism. Pride was the name of the game. Pride was the name of the Red Heads' game.

Rookies and second-year girls were taking basketball into the hotel rooms and were practicing on their arm fakes, ball handling, ball-spinning routines, and other things we did. Sometimes early in the morning you would see them out at the back of the hotels doing juggling and things. They were constantly trying to become great professional people. The law of dignity, as I, Coach Moore, called it, was to never sit on the floor during practice or anytime. Instead, you should remove yourself and sit on a seat and put your heart on your shoulder, so your endeavor with the All American Red Heads can be seen by people all over America. I said you must make people respect you as a person first, and then the rest is easy.

The Red Heads established no booking agency and no advanced publicity personnel, just Mr. Olson and then later me, Orwell Moore. The public demanded to see the All American Red Heads. There was a magical magnitude of booking. The All American Red Heads were a great source of fundraising—women's basketball at its best—and developed a legacy for their players and coaches that will last forever. We did fundraisers for all types of associations: church groups, PTAs, Lions Clubs, veterans groups, American Legion groups, and many more all over the country who wanted to raise funds for special projects.

We played to as many full houses as any team of our time. We set attendance records all over the sports world, and some still exist today. We had a great rapport with people attending the games. The All American Red Heads wanted to prove that women could play basketball. We had to do it—full court against men. Our main objective was to dispel the social, medical, and biblical beliefs of society that women couldn't play basketball. Even if we had to do it with five players, full court, and by men's rules.

We were selling basketball everywhere we went. The story of the All American Red Heads was an unfolding adventure of hard work and dreams; an eternal schedule of long hours of planning, visualizing, practicing, and perfecting our game; and an ongoing journey into sports legends.

The story of the All American Red Heads is a love story about two people who built their lives on the All American Red Heads and spent the next fifty years in a thrilling adventure of women's basketball. What a story!

Who were these girls who played basketball for the All American Red Heads? They were young leaders in their communities, cheerleaders, basketball players, number one in the schools they attended—but they were more than that in their communities. They were church leaders. They were youth activities leaders. They were leaders in their communities, churches, and schools, and they were, of course, number-one basketball players in their schools. The All American Red Heads were not only gifted athletes but were also very smart. One year when we had two teams on the road, I signed sixteen seniors from high schools across America.

The Red Heads came to us from working families whose mothers wanted better lives for their daughters. The mothers had been so-called "community locked." Such a mother had grown up in the community she lived in. She had gotten married in the community she lived in, and she had raised a family in the community she lived in. But she wanted something better for her daughter. She wanted her daughter to have and raise a family—every mother wants that—but she wanted more. She wanted her daughter to be able to see America or a part of it that otherwise she would never see.

The Red Heads got each of these daughters, and I can tell you that the mothers were very important and very instructive to the Red Heads. The mothers were very instructive in talking to girls and getting them to sign the contracts. Mothers, you were our greatest recruiting tool! The girls that I was searching for really had a place in the communities that they lived in. These girls were promised jobs after graduation at the bank or in leading jobs in industry in their towns.

The magic phrase I used on the other girls was "basketball, travel, and pay." So that was the beginning of my successful recruiting period. Belief in God was an important thing to me. I really wasn't a person who pushed religion, but I believed in God, I believed in our country, I believed in the things that made our country great, and I wanted girls who knew something about God—if they belonged to the church, that was a plus in their favor. We must believe in God and all my girls did. Many of these players carried a small Bible or Testament with them when they came to play. As we moved across the country, as we did many times, we did not have time to go to Sunday school or church. Some Sunday mornings we had a short distance to go that afternoon or that night to play ball. The girls knew that because we had our schedule, and we talked about it every day. So they would get up early the next morning and call the ministers of the churches of their choice and explain that they didn't have any churchgoing clothes—they only had slacks and blouses—and they would ask if they could come and be a part of the church services. I never heard of a minister turning them down. So the girls went to church, and the ministers welcomed them. They announced them and told the people that they were present and asked each girl to stand up and give her name and the town that she was from. That was great publicity. Being able to go to church and be recognized by the church people was a great thing.

A lot of times the church members would ask the girls if they would like to have lunch with them. The girls were very appreciative, but they knew they had to get back on the road to make it to their next game. They were so thrilled that the people invited them. As time went on, we met people who were becoming ministers and who had played basketball and sports in college. Quite often when we got to town, those ministers would be playing on the town team. They wanted to play against the girls. They were fun-loving people who liked to show to the community that they wanted to give a helping hand in the activities. And they were fun; I tell you, they were something else. They did a great job, and we want to thank those ministers for promoting the game and making it possible in their communities. That was very important to the people and to the ministers. Any time a minister announced at his church that he would be playing at our game, you could bet that most of the members of his church would be there.

What is an All American Red Head? Well, I will tell you what one of our great players, Barb Hostert of Mikeny, Illinois, said. She is the little lady who said, "Mom, I'm going to play basketball with the All American Red Heads." That was the first basketball game the girl had ever seen, and as a youngster she attended Camp Courage for four years. Then she finished high school and played on the high school team, and, of course, the Red Heads adopted her. She played as an outstanding star for five years for the All American Red Heads. I'll tell you now what she wrote that the All American Red Heads were and are.

(Note: Just prior to the completion of this book, Barb Hostert passed away, having suffered from multiple sclerosis for some time. She told Brenda Koester, who is featured in the chapter on family, that "I am not mad with God because he has allowed me to live my dream by playing for the Red Heads." So it is more than appropriate to include this quote by her and also fitting that Orwell should choose it to represent the spirit and identity of the Red Heads.)

An All American Red Head is not just an average basketball player on an average team with an average performance. She is a very colorful magician on the court who is ready to play basketball with authority, aggressiveness, and mental toughness. She is a basketball wizard with master deception. The moment that she lures her opponent into a trance, she will take advantage of the moment and quickly follow through with her attack; because of her polished play and experience, she will trust her next move. A Red Head will use individual ball handling, crisp passing, and ability to score before the opponent even has a chance to realize just what has transpired. A Red Head will keep the opponent on his toes. A Red Head makes the game so interesting that the crowd is in awe at her spectacular performance. An All American Red Head takes pride in being a member of such an elite organization, known as the world champions all over the globe.

The Red Head learns to live by the four Ds: dedication, desire, discipline, and determination. She will understand the importance of the four Ds and the influence that they have on her everyday life. A Red Head doesn't just love to play or watch basketball. She demonstrates her love for the game with a passion when she speaks of the game, of her team, or of her organization. The Red Head values lessons that will last a lifetime. There is no *I* in team, as the familiar saying goes. It is the Red Heads organization's belief that you do not promote the star individual but rather a team full of stars. After all, they are all stars. It was persistent teamwork, skill, and finesse that made the Red Heads an awesome unit. A Red Head will never forget the strength that a team has from working together. An individual with the intention of being in the spotlight by herself for her own recognition and glory does not fit in and will eventually eliminate herself from the team. A Red Head is unselfish and will help her teammates look good without being asked. She is a very special person and will work tirelessly to be a dependable, unselfish teammate.

The Red Head will dress herself up with a good attitude. The public sees the confidence in her posture, speech, and expression. The audience attends the game to see champion foul shots, crisp passing, high-percentage field goals, good positions for rebounds, defense played like demons, and world-champion basketball players. The audience members walk away with memories for life when they see a fantastic team performance unlike that of any ordinary team. The fans leave with a lasting impression embedded in their hearts that will stay with them forever because of the excitement.

The Red Heads mesmerized audiences with such skill and finesse that the fans left the games with admiration, emotion, and respect for the players and team.

A Red Head will listen to her coach, welcome criticism, and play with perks. She plays with authority and composure and always tries her best to be the player her coach wants and knows she can be. A Red Head will improve herself by practicing her weaknesses and always striving for perfection, and she doesn't have to be reminded that mediocre play is not accepted. The Red Heads are my lifetime friends. They played a big part in my development as an athlete and a person. What an advantage to have teammates all over the world wherever you are. And wherever you travel, the Red Heads may be right around the corner.

What were some of the achievements of some of the All-American Red Heads? Well, the Red Heads proved that women could play basketball and that it was a great, clean, and healthy sport. They could play the game and prove that. The 1936–39 Red Heads were outstanding girls. They stormed America and proved that they could play. They played 150 games each year. Ole Olson was getting a great number of people wanting to see the Red Heads. There were two thousand sponsors wanting to sponsor the All-American Red Heads. They proved women could play basketball. They played every night and came home healthy doing it.

Now the next medical question was answered by some of these girls who got married and started families right away. One of the old medical wives' tales at that time was that if a woman engaged in athletics or competitive events, it could affect her ability to have children. The ladies proved right away that that was wrong! Well, most of society said that it would never last—it did last, and the Red Heads proved that women could play basketball against men's teams with no ill medical effects, and they did it for fifty years. So the health authorities had to relent.

Another thing was the religious issue of women playing sports. Many church authorities said that that was wrong. Some claimed that no girl could be a Christian and go out and play sports or wear uniforms that exposed her body to people—that no Christian girl would be able to do a thing like that and be accepted. They were wrong again, because ministers came and participated in our games. Great church members showed up to see us play. Once again we were tearing down the misunderstandings of society. Society, you've got to accept us! Here are fifty years on the road with the All-American Red Heads, and girls' basketball is one of the greatest games going today, professional, amateur, and scholastic.

No one did a better job at selling basketball than the All American Red Heads. Over the years the All American Red Heads have been watched by great stars of Hollywood, governors, and legislators from cities large and small. They came to the games and were impressed by the All-American Red Heads' ability to play basketball well and in a most interesting way. These governors and legislators (including some US senators, representatives, and mayors) came up to the Red Heads and thanked them right away for a wonderful performance.

Then there was a call for schools all over America to feature women's athletics and basketball. We think we had much to do with that. Then came the legislators who said the women should have the right to participate in school sports and have a budget. Half the money should go to women's athletics, and, of course, that was a big boost to the ladies of America. Up until that time, many ladies, women, and girls of America were not considered first-class citizens. They didn't get the same amount of money or instruction, but with Title IX the girls became first-class citizens along with the boys. So you can see that we feel we had an important influence on the legislators and people who wanted to give the girls a chance to play basketball. Once again we'd like to claim a part of that.

The All-American Red Heads were many things. They were a mood, a state of mind, a philosophy. They were as brisk as the wind off the Atlantic Ocean. They were as gentle as a breeze off the Pacific Ocean. They were a small town with one city light. They were like the concrete jungles of big cities. Red Heads were laughter and love. They had happiness and the songs of youth. The Red Heads were as American as the fiddle at a country dance. The Red Heads were the magic mixture of good female athletes. They were as American as a traffic jam, the junior prom, the Labor Day parade. The Red Heads were the red, white, and blue of the past. They boasted the hope of tomorrow, that women's and girls' basketball would become the great game it is today. The Red Heads' magic prevailed. The bottom line is that the All American Red Heads brought the exuberance of health, a keen sense of direction, a passion for playing basketball, and a willingness to dream. The All American Red Heads were as American as apple pie.

CHAPTER 9

The Swinging Sixties

● ● ●

Imagination has a great deal to do with winning.

—MIKE KRZYZEWSKI

CARAWAY BECAME THE HOME OFFICE of the Red Heads, and the small town was proud to call the team its own. One young man was particularly enamored with the idea of a professional women's basketball team operating right out of his own backyard. Ben Overman began his lifelong association with the Red Heads at the age of sixteen, doing a variety of jobs from creating posters to managing the mail. Growing up in Caraway, he and his family knew the Moores and shared the love of basketball. Ben himself was a pretty good athlete at Caraway High School, where Orwell coached. On graduation, Orwell offered the young Overman a chance to travel with the team, and in 1961 Overman became the official coach.

As coach, mentor, and manager, Ben continued the sporting and behavioral standards that Moore had set, but there was some adaptation to the Swinging Sixties. For example, later in the era, Overman talked about his attitude concerning players dating local men.

"A member of the Jaycees or somebody connected with sponsoring the game in town will want to take one of the girls out. OK with us, but I try to make inquiries. Don't make it sound like I'm watching over the players all the time, I'm not," said Ben to a reporter from the *Chicago Sun Times*.

He "quietly checked out" the man in question before giving his approval. By then, players were getting a little more latitude. Being on the road for months at a time and barely standing still was a single gal's life. It was glamorous, but it could also be lonely. It isn't surprising then that one of the players fell in love with the coach. They didn't date when on the road, but when the season ended in 1962, they spent the summer dating and were married by the time the season had resumed. They became the third coach-player, husband-and-wife team, and much like Butch Moore, Pat Overman was a leading figure on the team. Like Lorene Moore before her, Pat worked harder than anyone else, lest people get the wrong reason why she was on the court. Pat suggested that Orwell Moore liked the idea of the coach being married to one of the players; a single male coach could have presented problems.

Pat was the team captain and comedian, the Red Mason of her era. She admitted she was very happy to be married and liked the idea of settling down. She suggested that one of the biggest reasons that girls left the team was indeed to get married.

Pat said the players felt like celebrities wherever they went. They were courted by autograph seekers and the media. She recalled being invited on to the *Johnny Carson Show*:

One night, we flew up to New York from New Orleans to appear on the *Johnny Carson Show*. We spent the entire next day in the studio being interviewed and doing ball-handling routines with Johnny and his brother, Dick Carson, who was directing the show. After we finished we spent the rest of the time in the dressing room waiting to go on. We were all dressed in uniforms and had lots of fun with Johnny. Roy Clark, the country singer from *Hee Haw*, was on right before us, and he sang and talked over into our time. The director kept coming into our dressing room saying, "He needs to get off the stage!" But he didn't and we never got to go on. Anyway we were there, and they asked us to stay over, but we couldn't as we had games booked. We were very disappointed as were all our fans and families. Nonetheless, it was a great experience, and we were treated very well.

At the other end of the excitement scale, driving long distances could be very boring, and the girls tried all sorts of things to wake themselves up, like shadow boxing and running around the car. The girls were not allowed to drive, so the driver could also get tired. Pat told of one new recruit who was picked up in St. Louis and driven four hundred miles. She fell asleep in the backseat and when she awoke, she was aware that the car had stopped and that the driver was running around the car hitting himself in the head to keep himself alert.

Like the other coach's wife, Lorene "Butch" Moore, before her, Pat worked very hard to prove her worth.

"My first year was anything but memorable. I wasn't as great as I thought I was, and my skills did not compare to the veteran players who were already playing with the Red Heads. But I decided to tough it out, play when I got the chance, and learn as much as I could from the other players."

She was dedicated and patient and eventually assumed the comedienne role on the team.

"Although I had never seen myself in this type of role, it was a challenge that I wanted to accomplish. Being the comedienne meant that you had to be a very skilled, competent player to do all the tricks and get laughs from the crowd. After three years of working every summer and between games, I was given the chance to be the comedienne for the All American Red Heads. It taught me to not only have a better sense of humor, but also to continue to improve my skills and ball handling, which was essential."

Her husband, Ben, ran a well-organized ship. The team never missed a game, although one was postponed. The Red Heads were playing just outside New York City the night of the infamous blackout. They arrived at the gym to find no electricity, and the game had to be postponed. The Red Heads also played a game the day that John F. Kennedy was assassinated, but they didn't really want to. The crowd was subdued, and everyone, including the Red Heads, was much more interested in the coverage on the television than the game.

When Ben wasn't coaching, supervising, and mentoring the girls, he was also monitoring the crowd. Some organizations were better managers of the gate than others. In one *Chicago Sun Times* article Ben said this:

"Lions clubs are the best sponsors. If I look on my schedule and see that it's the Lions handling things in the next town, I relax a little. They're usually the older businessmen in a place, they know how to get things done. Groups like the Jaycees—they're great people but they're younger, often don't know the right people, sometimes they aren't really sure what it means to handle an event like this."

Ben had to respond to unexpected opportunities. In one town there was a tap on his shoulder. He turned around and saw one of the tallest girls he had ever seen. Her father said she was six feet eight inches tall and was interested in playing for the Red Heads. That night, Ben called Orwell, who told him to get a tape measure and find out how tall the girl really was. Ben was able to confirm her height, and the girl was soon on her way to basketball camp. Her name was Rosali Kashmitter.

Ben's Takeaways

I have learned what it means to listen effectively and how to take direction as well as what it means to be a team player.

I have learned what it means to face opponents who are stronger and more experienced and to come out a winner, wiser for having had the experience.

I have learned to love challenges and to incorporate changes in my life with enthusiasm and a desire to make the best possible out of each situation.

I love challenges, and I understand what it means to be dedicated, to believe in myself and others, and to know what giving 100 percent means.

One of the stars of the sixties was Jolene Ammons. She would go on to have a stellar career that lasted more than a decade, in which she scored more than twenty-five thousand points and won 1,848 of the 2,316 games she played.

At the beginning, however, not everything was auspicious. For one thing, she hated red hair.

"Every time I walked by that mirror I had to do a double take. Who is this strange person? In the beginning you will never know how much I disliked the red hair. After a couple of years it was second nature. Miss Clairol, Flame Red. I had forgotten my real hair color."

In her first game at Strawberry, Arkansas, Mr. Moore taught Jolene a valuable lesson. Up to that point in her career, Jolene had played mostly half court or only informally on a full court.

Mr. Moore kept yelling at me to play wide! Give the post player some working room. In my mind I was playing wide. Not good enough! After the half-time show Mr. Moore again asked if I knew where the corners of the court were. I replied, 'Yes, I do.' He told me to show him where they were. I pointed to all four corners. Still not good enough! He actually had me jog to each corner. Now here I am supposed to be a professional basketball player, and I have to show the owner of the team the corners of the court!

Jolene learned to be an outstanding ball handler, a combination of her own natural talent and input from the coaches and Lorene Moore. Each pass was given a special name.

"I could refer to a side drop kick, butt pass, or spin drop, and we knew what was coming next."

It took a lot of practice to develop and maintain these skills.

"Almost every day after we had checked into the motel, I would grab three balls and head out to the parking lot. I did a lot of chasing before I learned," said Jolene.

But practice made perfect, and Jolene got to use the skills in front of a national audience.

"We were on the *Mike Douglas Show*, and Betty White was a guest. Betty White was an actress, an animal-rights activist, and a comedienne regarded as one of the pioneers of television. I was thrilled when asked to spin the ball and place it on Betty's finger. She was a very warm and friendly person."

Homesickness was also a part of the story of the kid from southern Georgia.

"We played in Mickey Childress's home town on Christmas Day. This was my first Christmas away from home, also my first white Christmas (it never snowed in southeast Georgia). Mickey's folks had us over for Christmas to exchange gifts, and that was fun, but when the carolers came around, I was like Old Faithful. While at the laundromat, I decided to phone my folks, and as soon as my mother said hello, we started to cry. We cried for about five minutes before we could talk."

One memorable game for Jolene was against an all-black team and at the time, interracial games were unheard of.

"The sponsor had a police escort every place we went. They were real nice guys to play against." The Red Heads lost by two points.

Another girl from Georgia was Becky Harp, who played for the Red Heads from 1965–69.

"I don't know how or why he found me," she said about Orwell Moore's approach to her, "but when I received the letter from him telling me all about the Red Heads (whom I had never heard of), I was elated and ready to go. I think I accepted right away for fear he may have my name by mistake!"

Like the rest of the Red Heads, Becky was the supreme team player, but it's another memory that she cherishes most.

"The greatest satisfaction for me came about two to three minutes into the game. The look on the guys' faces when they realized, 'These girls can really play—we'd better get to work.' It happened a lot. We truly earned their respect. By the time they realized we were there to play ball, we were usually out in front, and they would have to buckle down and play hard, and that was even better for us because our plays worked much better when we could counterattack."

Becky fondly remembers being featured on the *Linkletter Show* and meeting Don Knotts, Red Skelton, and a lot of other celebrities. Becky also recounts the impact of another change in the Red Heads organization at the time—the introduction of a new coach, who was needed now that there were three Red Heads units in action. This coach was in a similar mold as Orwell Moore and Ben Overman.

The first similarity was that Jack Moore was married. Jack himself cut an imposing physical figure, which contrasted to that of his wife, Bettye, who according to Becky, "might have just made it to five feet tall." Unlike Butch and Pat, however, Bettye was not a basketball player—but she was a team player.

"She was very feisty, but she was always there for the girls," recalled Becky. "And she was a wiz at managing the business part of the operation—booking, accounts, and stuff like that." Part of that motivation might have come from the fact that her husband, Jack, was Orwell's brother, so this wasn't just any coaching position; they were running the family business.

Becky recalled that Jack was a very high-energy and fun-loving person. "He was like a father and brother to us. He worked us hard and ensured that we were at the top of our game. But he also reminded us that we were there to make memories and have fun."

And Jack was always insistent that wherever possible, the team took time out to visit the great sights of the areas they were passing through.

"We saw so much of the great country. That was a huge perk of being a Red Head," said Becky.

But like his brother, Jack was demanding. If you didn't execute well on the floor, he let you know about it.

I remember that look. His eyebrows were knitted in a frown, and his lips pursed; you knew you had messed up.

Being Orwell's brother made a difference. I think Jack would have been just the same coach but because he was involved in the entire organization, I think it made him and Bettye mindful of the big picture.

Carolyn Grantham was also another Georgia girl on the 1966 team. She was just seventeen.

"People ask me why I left at such an early age to play professional basketball. I tell them that was the year I grew up. I grew up to become a better person and learned to get along with others. We played seven nights a week and sometimes twice on Sunday. I stayed with six other girls in a different motel each night. We had our own personalities, and we had to adapt."

Carolyn played just one year and was married soon after she left the team.

Brenda Moon was another star of the late-sixties team. But she almost never made it. At six feet two inches, she excelled in her local high school team in the Nashville area and got a lot of recognition and awards. But Brenda was shy, didn't like the limelight, and became particularly reclusive when she got some prank calls after getting some media attention. So it was no surprise that when she got a call from someone claiming to be the owner of a professional women's basketball team, Brenda hung up the phone.

"Shortly, the phone rang again, but I refused to answer it and told my dad that someone was playing a bad trick on me. Eventually, my dad answered the call to try to put a stop to it. Fortunately for me, Orwell Moore was persistent, and my dad took the time to listen to what the coach had to say. Otherwise who knows what path my life and future would have taken."

Shyness and the idea of being away from her family almost prevented Brenda from showing up at all. However, in the end, she said, "It would be too embarrassing to quit after all the local publicity I got on signing my first contract with the Red Heads."

Brenda needn't have worried about being lonely and isolated. The girls lived and worked together on everything. Even her first Christmas away wasn't as bad as she thought. The girls even got a Christmas tree for their hotel room. She told her teammates that every Christmas, Santa filled a sock that she left hanging by her bed with goodies for her to find the next day.

"When I woke up on Christmas morning, one of my gym socks was stuffed full of treats and hung on the headboard of the bed. Among the more prized items in that sock were a leftover hamburger and cold fries from the night before!"

Brenda eloquently describes the meaning of the Red Heads in her life. Her shyness and self-doubt were erased. Through radio shows, media interviews, and public speaking, "I learned that you can overcome your doubts and fears by planning, practicing, and executing."

While raised to believe she could achieve anything, Brenda said she was "from a culture and time where males were the supposed leaders and dominant forces in society, and females were, at least to some degree, less capable, functioning more in subordinate roles. I began to believe that women could compete in a man's world."

Brenda didn't just use her Red Heads experience to challenge gender stereotypes. She used it to challenge all stereotypes.

She was highly talented at programming the early computers and headed down that path even though those jobs were traditionally male-dominated positions. After graduating from business college, she faced another challenge; she didn't have the required four-year degree. What irked her more was that the degree didn't have to be in anything relevant to computers—employers were insisting on a four-year degree.

"Armed primarily with the confidence that I gained through my Red Heads experiences, I set my mind on getting that first computer job and prove all those human-resources folks wrong about people who didn't have a four-year degree. A major insurance company in Nashville gave me my first opportunity, and I have been working with computers and automation in the insurance industry ever since."

That's thirty-plus years.

Brenda has also risen to senior executive positions (like CEO and assistant vice-president) within an industry that tends to be male dominated. She owes her success to her experiences as a Red Head.

She puts her success down to "having confidence in myself regardless of the competition or the playing field; the value of planning, practicing, and executing; the importance of true teamwork."

Another player from the late sixties, Therese Bergeron expressed the same sentiments. Therese might just be the shortest Red Head ever—at five feet three inches tall. Despite her height she was a star all through school, but then came graduation and a lot of sadness.

"Women's college basketball was not very popular in the sixties. Scholarships were almost unheard of," she recalled.

One rainy November night in 1968, she went to see the Red Heads, and she was awestruck. After the game she accosted the players and anyone who seemed to be associated with them with endless questions about how to make the team. The rest is history.

As a shorter player, Therese had to learn to overcome some serious disadvantages.

I knew I had a struggle ahead of me. However, with the proper coaching and new techniques, height was no longer an obstacle but a challenge. I learned quickly to use my speed and agility to maneuver around and under the taller players.

In years to come I applied the same theory each day of my life. Every problem or dilemma that crossed my path became a challenge I knew I could overcome.

Another player who made an impact around this time was Carolyn Gooch (now Hix). Carolyn was listed as six feet three inches tall and played center. She didn't keep track of her stats but told the story of her most productive night in a game played in Michigan. She scored thirty-eight points, almost twice her average. "Everything was going in," she said. Carolyn was quick to point out that in her position, rebounding was more important than scoring. However, there was something that might have been more important than both scoring and rebounding, and it's not on the stat sheet.

"I want you on my team because you have sparkle," Orwell told Carolyn. When she looked at him quizzically, he replied, "One day, you'll know what I am talking about."

Sparkle. It characterized the Red Heads and made them who they were. It was the quality that elevated the team to more than just a girls' basketball team. The girls weren't just physically fit, supremely well coached, and talented. They had passion. They had pizzazz. They had style. They had class. They had femininity.

The Red Heads weren't tomboys. They wore makeup. They did their hair. They dressed well whenever they went out. They always looked good. They delighted in being women. They didn't just shoot and rebound. They winked, flashed smiles, and even flirted.

"A lot of the guys on opposing teams would tell us, 'You're not at all what we expected,'" said Carolyn. "I think they were expecting masculine women with few feminine qualities. Boy, were they wrong!"

When they first entered town and people didn't know who they were, the Red Heads were often not seen as a basketball team, even though the limo had that fact emblazoned right across it in bold letters.

"A lot of the time, when we got out of the car, people would ask us, 'Are y'all a band?'"

They saw the sparkle.

The sparkle probably surprised the fans too, the vast majority of whom came to root on the Red Heads.

"It was natural for me to interact with the fans. I blew them kisses, chatted with them, even flirted with them. I was a live wire out on the court," said Carolyn.

For Carolyn several aspects of the Red Heads experience stood out.

"The opportunity to travel was an amazing, once-in-a-lifetime thing. The sisterhood was incredible. I loved those girls, and it is hard to imagine being in a closer group," Carolyn admitted. "Meeting a lot of interesting people, doing the radio and TV shows, and constantly being in the limelight were great experiences."

Did she and her teammates realize the impact they were having?

"There were so many young girls at our games who were in awe. We would wait until we had given every last autograph and the building was empty, so we knew that we were impacting them. But not in a million years did we think we were having a such an impact or that one day we would be in the Hall of Fame," said Carolyn.

Carolyn left the team after two seasons to get married. She comments that there was no time for a personal life when on the road with the Red Heads. Her personality and emotional intelligence put her in good a position in her career, which featured stints as a makeup artist, a sales manager, a payroll supervisor, and the general manager of two nightclubs.

"I was interviewing a young lady one day for a job. She had a great personality, and then I suddenly realized what Orwell meant by sparkle. I'm not going to take credit for it—it's just the way I am," said Carolyn.

"Other than the birth of my three children, Jennifer, Kameron, and Bryan, the Red Heads team was the greatest thing that happened in my life," Carolyn admitted.

And talking of children, daughter Jennifer was a stand-out basketball player, and one granddaughter, Aspen, thirteen, is also a great player with a lot of potential. And they have sparkle.

Players like Brenda and Therese learned resilience, confidence, and courage on their way to facing the challenges they faced in life as women. One can only imagine the number of young girls and women among the millions who watched the Red Heads play throughout the sixties who were similarly inspired by the exploits of those redheaded girls on the court. Times were a-changing, and the Red Heads were leading the charge.

CHAPTER 10

Basketball: The Magnificent Game

Orwell Moore

● ● ●

Basketball is a game of fast changes of pace, multiple means of attack, multiple guises of defense, baffling surprises, confusing ruses, wily questing, skillful strategies, vicious charges, fickle diversions, and fierce individual competition.

—ORWELL MOORE

BASKETBALL IS A GAME OF fast starts, abrupt turns, clever twists, elusive spins, clever deceptions, sharp angles, synchronized thinking, sudden stops, magic faking, peripheral disguises, camouflaged chatter, misleading decoys, precise timing, constant changing of situations, rapid shift of player responsibility, split-second judgments, percentage-wise team play, wise use of individual and team fundamentals, an ever awareness of time "stabilizers," constant attack, furious loose-ball clashes, fast changes of pace, multiple means of attack, multiple guises of defenses, baffling surprises, confusing ruses, wily guessing, skillful strategy, vicious charging, fickle diversions, fierce individual competition, swift changes from offense to defense and vice versa, brilliant and magnificent offensive attacks, and dogged and determined defense. It is a game of abrupt reverses, fierce drives, subtle feints, quick changes in direction, skillful maneuvers, tactful strategies, tenacious and unrelenting aggressiveness, a culmination of hundreds of individual player-to-player contests, high excitement, hysterical fan participation, terrific body-energy assumption, an ever-aware overloading of consciousness, deliberate "spreading and funneling" movements, and ever-changing patterns, situations, area, space, time number, angles, advantages, and percentages.

Basketball is magnificent in offensive attack, dogged and determined in defense. Basketball is a game of high endeavor and tremendous patterns of hope-faith achievements. Basketball is a game of skilled discipline, studious dedication, and commitment to the challenges the game offers. The will to be the very best you can be, the will to be a winner. The will to win!

Basketball is a game of marvelous anticipation, a game of many momentous moments of truth. Basketball is a game that offers accelerated high living to all its players. There are no static situations in the great game of basketball.

Basketball is a game of geometry, trigonometry, and plain mathematics. Basketball is a game that has many patterns of time limitations. Basketball is a game of principle limitations for every player: you must play the game by the rules.

Basketball presents strong, firm self-control. Basketball is a game of discipline. Basketball has fewer animal instincts than football. In football you have the opportunity to hit back. In basketball you can only take the disciplined way out. You can throw the ball in from out of bounds or shoot the foul shots. The disciplined way to hit back is to make a good pass in or make the foul shots. Hit the shots, make the pass in, and hit back with self-control and discipline.

Basketball lifts its players out of the low, the mire of animal instincts, the average, the danger, and the monotony more than any other game I know. It offers many times over the chance for its skilled performer to soar in soul-lifting experience high above the din of the crowd.

Basketball presents a picture of spiritual endeavor—to the discipline of the player, to the task of game preparation, and to the true belief of the team and coach that you can attain pinnacles of success in the game plan that you will employ.

Basketball certainly is a game of life, with all the sins of humanity showing their ugly heads, such as selfishness, greed, dishonesty, gossip, self-centeredness, egotism, and poor sportsmanship. But basketball affords the opportunity and the situations for its players to meet those horrible qualities and drive them away with direct and concise action that portrays honesty, hard work, and dedication. It requires a disciplined and unselfish concentration on being a better player and a better student. Every great player develops a great passion for playing basketball. The game of basketball must put a high respect on the player's honor, honesty and the big effort. Egotism has been lost. A winner is looking at her teammates and coaches through her heart and not through her eyes. Basketball can point with pride to its great performers. Basketball can point with pride to its royalty. Basketball can point with pride to its every game's drama and pageantry.

Basketball is the magnificent game. It's Friday night, and gymnasiums, arenas, and sport halls are lit up all over the United States. "This is basketball night," people say. "Let's go to the local high school game." The gymnasium is packed to capacity and is overflowing. There is a rampant anticipation in the crowd—this banner-waving, cap-wearing, T-shirted mass shouting good-natured banter across the gym to the opposing team's fans and followers. The wild excitement is beginning to rise. The teams come on the floor for a pregame warm up. A thunderous ovation greets the competitors in a tremendous surge of pride and loyalty. Now comes the introduction of the players—then the starting five—and then a sudden hush comes over this mass of humanity—what wild anticipation. Can our center get the tip, or will the opposing team control the ball? The crowd is in a momentary frenzy, in a wild frame of hope and anguish. Then comes the storm—no matter who gets the tip, this wildly enthusiastic crowd is in the game.

Basketball, the magnificent game, is exploring and exploding the talents of the players on the floor. But it also creates a frenzy of excitement that permeates the home crowd as well as the opposing team's fans.

As the game progresses, interrupted only by the shrill whistle of the referees, the fans become totally engrossed in the game, dying with fouls called and cheering loudly for any advantage gained. The concentration of the ebb and the flow of the game is great as the players charge up and down the court.

The home team is behind, and the time left on the clock is working against the home team. The home team is losing, so every move and every pass is more important than ever. The anxiety level is next to panic. This can't be happening. The opposing fans are living it up, and the clock is ticking; suddenly the whistle blows—the home team has tied the score! The clock shows ten seconds left in the game, and the opposing team has taken possession of the ball and called time out. But in a blur the home team now has possession of the ball and called time out. They wait for the whistle and throw the ball in toward the girl. There is a skirmish, and Jack or John or Jill or Lill comes up with the ball and puts a shot up that fills the net. Home team wins! Home team wins!

CHAPTER 11

Camp Courage

● ● ●

Success is never final, failure is never fatal. It's courage that counts.

—JOHN WOODEN

WHILE BEN OVERMAN WAS COACHING the team, Orwell Moore still did most of the recruiting, convincing potential recruits' parents of the values and opportunities of the Red Heads. And as the fame of the Red Heads spread, with now three teams on the road, there was more interest in becoming a Red Head and more need to recruit and train players.

Moore had been running camps out of other people's schools and places but really wanted a place of his own. In his own words, he said the following:

"The idea of having a basketball camp was a magnificent obsession of mine. I was very much aware of the different camps in Oklahoma, summer camps for students to learn basketball. I wanted to have a camp somewhere that would be permanent."

Moore started his search for his own campsite. He found a place in Lepanto, Arkansas, but the deal was too complicated. Then there was a place near Hardy, Oklahoma, that had a big water wheel and a motel, but Moore could never find out who actually owned the property and whether it was even for sale. Then he read in the *Commercial Appeal*, a Memphis-based paper, that a place called Camp Courage was for sale. Moore contacted the realtor and found out that the owner was a Mr. McHouston from West Memphis, Arkansas.

"Camp Courage was started by Mr. O'Dell and some men in the military," recalled Orwell later. "They wanted to take care of delinquent boys. It depended on donations. Elvis Presley donated $40,000 to build the swimming pool; he also donated a card table with barrel chairs."

O'Dell later abandoned the camp when the delinquent boys became unruly, and the project became unmanageable. That's when Mr. McHouston bought it.

I went down to look at it and fell in love with it. The major problem was that it didn't have any roads coming in from the front gate, and everything was grown over. Lorene was for it, but she realized how much work it would take to get the camp ready.

We stopped by the camp and stayed overnight. We found a fishing pole and caught a big catfish. That sold Lorene on it.

Camp Courage had 343 acres of pine-covered hills, two large lakes, barrack-type housing, bathhouses, showers, and a large mess hall. Deer, wild turkey, and beavers were just some of the wildlife that roamed the camp.

The summer camp would primarily be used to teach girls basketball skills but could also be used as a way of assessing potential Red Heads talent. Now, instead of the Moores having to roam the country looking for talent, the talent would come to them.

They kept the name Camp Courage and ran the first program in the summer of 1971. Within a couple of years, it was a premier sports destination for boys and girls, with instruction and training in a variety of activities. The poster for the camp in 1974 offered the following activities: "Emphasis on basketball, other activities softball, volleyball, tennis, swimming, track, and fishing." There were also "special activities, intra-mural games, camp picnic, church night, stunt night, all-star games, and a special award night."

Camp Courage offered "the finest instruction in fundamentals and basic skills in these sports as well as "Personal, individual instructions—individual techniques as well as team work."

One immediate advantage of the camp was that some of the Red Heads could run the activities, thus providing them with a year-round income. Until then, Red Heads players had been off during the summer and not getting paid. In 1974, along with Lorene "Butch" Moore, who had the title of assistant director and instructor, there were five featured Red Heads as coaches: Jolene Ammons, Charlotte Adams, Wanda England, Cheryl Clark, Jack Moore, as well as Pat and Ben Overman.

The camp activities typically ran from mid-June to the end of August, during the Red Heads' off-season. Of course, Coach Moore had his usual motivational message for potential camp attendees. To the young men he wrote this:

Camp Courage offers a motivation program that starts young athletes to think like a champion—work like a champion—play like a champion—live like a champion.

A player is good if he executes the fundamentals correctly—a player is great if he executes the fundamentals and with finesse—and a team is only as good as the fundamentals it executes. There are no shortcuts to fundamental payoffs.

Let Camp Courage help you become a great performer. If you are in the sixth grade or a college graduate, we can help you.

There was also a rider to the teamwork and mental skills instruction.

"Each player will be guided in instruction by the Basketball Rules of the State they will compete in," a testimony to the varied rules that did indeed exist at the time.

Lorene "Butch" Moore remembers

Camp Courage was exciting. It was something that we wanted to give to the young people of America. It was a great dream of Orwell's to touch young people and help them understand the game and what playing basketball could do for you. Not just winning and losing but getting ready for life.

Camps were a week long, though you could sign up for multiple weeks. The weekly rate in 1974 was eighty-five dollars but fifteen dollars extra if you wanted an air-conditioned room, which might have been preferable in the height of the Mississippi summer.

Meals were served in the large mess hall, where campers and coaches dined together. Camp doctors were on twenty-four-hour call, and the nearest hospital was just thirty minutes away. The camp was closed to the public. No camper was allowed to leave unless he or she was with a supervised group.

Despite the availability of instruction in different sports and the fact that the camp was open to boys, the main emphasis was on girls' basketball.

Here was Orwell's message to the "young ladies" who were interested in the camp:

Concentration of instruction to each individual will be the primary concern for our basketball camp.

Coaches that send girls to Camp Courage Basketball School will get a Report mailed directly to them at the end of the session— so that each coach will know what we have been working on—and a progress Report will be attached.

To The High School Graduates—I am able to offer 4 Full Athletic Scholarships—10 Part Time Scholarships and several Academic Scholarships—ALL to full accredited Colleges that play Girls basketball.

To High School Graduate, College Girl or Working Girl— that is interested in playing AAU Basketball—I know all of the Major Coaches in AAU Basketball and can arrange a try-out with the Team of your choice.

To young Olympic Hopefuls—Camp Courage Basketball camp plans to work toward a program that will make a definite contribution to the U.S.A. Team in the Olympics.

To the Young Lady—that is a High School or College Student that seeks to play Professional Basketball with a Girls Professional Team. You will be given every opportunity to be properly presented to the Professional group of your choice, and arrange a try-out with the team.

What in the world is going on? Women's college basketball scholarships? A girls' Olympic team? Athletic scholarships for women?

The fact was that the world had just changed. For almost forty years the Red Heads had championed the cause of women's basketball in particular and women's sports in general. They had challenged convention, undermined stereotypes, and completely changed the perception of women in sports and beyond. Their time had come, and now the world had changed in very significant ways.

CHAPTER 12

The Sparkling Seventies

● ● ●

As a result of Title IX, and a new generation of parents
who want their daughters to have the opportunities
they never had, women's sports have arrived.

—SHERYL SWOOPES

THE 1970S WERE A REMARKABLE decade for the Red Heads. Not only did they continue their miraculous feats on the court, racking up a win-loss record of 188–13 one year, they also continued to get national attention, being featured in a major *Sports Illustrated* article in 1974. And two years earlier, in 1972, President Nixon signed legislation that would transform female participation in sports, though few realized how much of an impact Title IX would have at the time.

The May 6, 1974, *Sports Illustrated* piece was written by William Johnson and Nancy Williamson and neatly summarized the history of the Red Heads as well as following the team on a typical road trip. There were several great quotes by Orwell Moore, who was interviewed at length, and these interviews gave some insight into how Orwell ran the organization as a whole.

For example, Moore explained the reason why no one, not even the girls themselves, were given the schedule more than thirty days in advance.

"We have to give them their routes so their folks can write to them but we never tell them beyond each month and they are generally sworn to secrecy about the schedule. If they told some reporter where they're playing, he might print the whole schedule in his paper and then some other attraction—donkey basketball, Gospel singers, some other basketball teams—could see it and set up a date in the same town a week or two ahead of the Red Heads. That would kill us dead. There's only so much entertainment money around."

Moore also shared his secret to the Red Heads business success. By teaming up with local fundraising charities, like the Lions Club, and generating money for the host communities, many expenses were avoided. As Moore explained:

"If you wanted to book into the Memphis Mid-South Coliseum it'd cost say, $1000 to rent, $250 for insurance, pay for ticket attendants, pay for the union men who turn off the lights, pay for the scoreboard keeper, pay for the referees. Then there'd be $600 to $700 to buy ads in the Memphis papers and twice that amount to buy ads on TV. It costs us only $140,000 a year to run the Red Heads organization."

Moore also made a point of mentioning the Harlem Globetrotters.

"I make it a point never to mention the Harlem Globetrotters, but when they claim to have originated many of the tricks that the All-American Red Heads actually began, then I feel I must speak out." Orwell also added, "The Globetrotters bring their own opponents along, we don't know who we're gonna play from night to night."

When asked about some of his recollections about the Red Heads, Orwell talked about the early days soon after he had come aboard in 1948.

We sometimes played in mighty shabby facilities, in church basements and on dance floors. We played once in an old factory in New Britain, Connecticut, where there was such a bend in the floor I couldn't see my team at the other end. We played on a skating rink once in New Castle, Pa. One place I remember was so dim they had to have small boys lying around the rafters holding little Aladdin's lanterns.

One night the lights went out due to an ice storm and we played by cars shining their headlights through the doors and windows so we didn't have to give the crowd their money back.

During his interviews with the *SI* writers, Orwell also emphasized another perk of being a Red Head.

Being a Red Head gives a girl a brand of appeal that she never had before. She goes home after a year of being a pro basketball player and she's gonna have guys calling her that she never knew before. My girls marry the Number one eligible bachelor in their communities; banker's son, rich ones with lots of dough, family dough.

The girls get married a lot. I sometimes call this the All-American Matrimonial Bureau.

Orwell also emphasized that through this fame, "they also get the best jobs when they go home."

Now it just so happened that the team that *SI* followed in the spring of 1974 consisted of several players who were, or would become, Red Heads legends.

First there was Jolene Ammons, who had switched her player's jersey for the coach's—and the chauffeur's—hat. Actually, Jolene hadn't quite traded in her jersey and also wore a number of hats. Sure, she was now at the wheel of the massive limo—now named Big Whitey—that transported the team cross the country. She was additionally described, however, as not just the player-coach and chauffeur but also "den mother, money collector, and road accountant."

At the time of the story, Jolene was thirty-two, but that didn't stop *SI* from writing that "she would probably be a star on any women's national team in the world, despite her age." In fact, the Basketball Hall of Fame in Springfield, Massachusetts, has asked for her jersey to be displayed there alongside stars of the era Wilt Chamberlain and Jerry West. It hangs there proudly today.

"I started playing basketball in the fourth grade and the girl next door took dancing lessons. Every afternoon she'd walk off her front porch with her tutu and I'd walk off mine with my basketball. She got to be Miss Georgia and I got to be a Red Head," Jolene told the *SI* writers.

Donna "Spanky" Losier from Gorham, New Hampshire, was five feet five inches tall and described as a comedienne and entertainer. Sound familiar? She spent a lot of her time traveling in Big Whitey by singing and playing the guitar.

"She burbles jokes…and helps pass the miles by singing in a sweet, clear voice, accompanied by her guitar. She is given to spurts of laughter and frequent exuberant I-Love-life eruptions about her role as a Red Head," said the *SI* story.

"Donna Losier is in a constant state of delight. She knows the words to 200 songs, can do imitations of everyone from Jonathan Winters to Richard Nixon, often snaps out of a sound sleep giggling and tossing out lines like, 'Hey, they say fish is brain food. Let's have a whale for lunch.'"

Spanky was indeed the team comedienne, on the court as well as off it. So she was a great ball handler and dribbler, a fine outside shooter, and, according to *SI*, "a notably unselfish passer."

How did she go from Donna to Spanky?

"In 1968 Coach Moore was traveling with us in the Red Heads limo on a trip to Little Rock. I was playing my guitar, laughing and hamming it up. That's when he said to me, 'You know, you remind me of Spanky on the *Little Rascals*. Spanky, that's a good name for you.'"

Spanky played for eleven years, featured in 1,885 games, and scored 20,721 points.

"I received a citation from the governor of New Hampshire when I played in my hometown. I met and played against Fergie Jenkins, met Hank Aaron when he attended our game in Atlanta, played against the San Francisco 49ers and the Denver Broncos. I played in all the states except Alaska and Hawaii and played in Mexico and Canada, too. I received keys to many cities, and we were also featured in books, magazines, and newspaper articles and appeared on national television."

And you know that Spanky loved every second of it.

Another member of the team was Cheryl Clark from Wetmore, Michigan, "six feet tall and exceedingly graceful." Cheryl, the daughter of a schoolteacher, "wears tinted spectacles and looked almost scholarly, a writer of many letters during the long periods in the limousine."

Cheryl was quoted as saying this: "I love basketball because I like the feel of running, the constant motion, the instantaneous decisions. Your mind stays active and that is stimulating."

The article continued, "Cheryl glides so smoothly when she plays that the game seems almost gentle. She has perfected a driving shot from beyond the free throw line that opponents never block, and which she seldom misses. This is her fifth year with the Red Heads; last year she performed with the other unit and it won 96 games in a row and finished the year with a 199–6 record."

Two mainstays of the Red Heads at this time were an oddity—they were twins, identical twins. They were tall, six feet one, and played in the post position, often switching, which surely confused their opponents.

Lynnette and Lynnea Sjoquist were from Cannon Falls, Minnesota. They grew up on a farm and were used to working hard. The twins were, of course, used to doing things together, and when they saw the Red Heads play in their hometown, they were both equally awestruck.

The twins excelled at volleyball and softball as well as basketball. Their mom had played high school basketball, and they had competitive brothers.

"We'd have our main meal at noon, and then Dad would take a nap, and we'd go out with our three brothers and play basketball on a concrete court behind the barn," said Lynnea.

After the twins spoke with Coach Ben Overman, they were invited to the summer camp—Camp Courage.

Lynnette recalled that certain members of their family weren't sure what to make of the twins heading off to a place where they knew no one.

"My brother thought we were nuts. My mom was very supportive, however, and she convinced Dad to let us chase our dream," recalled

Lynnette. "Mr. Moore picked us up in Memphis, and then we drove to this camp that seemed like it was in the middle of a forest."

The twins from Minnesota played together on the Red Heads for two years before Orwell split them up. At the time there were three teams on the road, and Moore needed to balance them out and needed taller players on a different unit. The split was quite a shock for the twins.

"Up to that point we had done everything together," recalled Lynnette. "We even lost the same tooth at the same time!"

Lynnea said, "We actually took all the same college classes together. So it was definitely an adjustment to play on a separate team."

Lynnea went to play with the Famous Red Heads.

"The team I played with was less experienced in that there was only one other veteran on the team besides me, Rhonda—the rest were rookies. A seasoned veteran joined us in January, so that helped considerably."

The schedule might have been easier—they only lost six games the entire year—but there were other duties that needed to be undertaken.

"Rhonda and I assumed all the responsibilities of managing money, travel, car repairs, and, of course, the rookies."

In addition, Lynnea became an auto mechanic.

"I learned how to change out an axle on our Pontiac. It was a stretch limo but did not have dual axles like the Oldsmobiles had. Therefore, we actually carried a spare axle with bearings pressed on, which of course was more weight and allowed for less luggage space."

Lynnea decided to retire after her fourth season. However, she was soon lured out of retirement by Orwell Moore in January of 1978. And Lynnea was soon thrust back into the challenge because of her height.

"The most notable fact that year was that we had a player who was six feet ten. She was the tallest Red Head ever. It was a struggle for her to even fit in our car. She at least got the bed to herself. However, one of the results of advertising a tall Red Head was that competing teams would recruit players that were just as tall or taller. Well, Susan was only really strong enough to play a couple minutes—so guess who got to defend the big guys?" said Lynnea.

Lynette had retired by then. She played through 1977 and then had a stint as a player with the Minnesota Fillies in the newly formed Women's Basketball League (WBL). After she finished playing, she worked in the front office for a while. Since then Lynnette has had a variety of technology jobs but has also worked as a broadcaster doing color commentary for the University of Minnesota women's basketball team.

In a piece that appeared in 2010 on the website www.startribune.com, Lynnette was quoted as saying this:

"I got to meet some unbelievable people who came to our games, like Hank Aaron. I got to play against people like Joe Theisman. That's one hand. The other hand is the overall experience to me; carrying the banner for women's sports. That drove it for me."

As mentioned, Lynnette played in a new women's basketball league, the WBL. It is hardly surprising that Orwell Moore was trying to establish such a league. In fact, he had set out the rules and regulations for league operations and had numerous discussions with interested parties. However, rumor has it that unbeknownst to him, some of those interested parties had less-than-savory reputations with connections to gambling, and their presence discouraged others from collaborating in Orwell's projects, instead backing rival alternatives.

Gambling connections also featured in another version of the battle of the sexes.

In 1973, the self-promoting former tennis ace Bobby Riggs boasted that women's tennis was inferior and that he, even at the age of fifty-five, could beat the current female stars. He challenged Billie Jean King, but after she refused, Riggs played the top-rated woman at the time, the Australian Margaret Court. On Mother's Day, May 13, 1973, Riggs defeated Court 6–2, 6–1. The match was watched by five thousand fans but generated huge media interest, and this led to Billie Jean King accepting Riggs's invitation to play a five-set match. The match, dubbed "the battle of the sexes," was played in the Astrodome in Houston on September 20, 1973. The winner would collect $100,000. King won 6–4, 6–3, 6–3. Despite the subsequent inquest into why Riggs played so poorly, including some suggestions that he bet heavily on the game and was in with the mob, King's win marked a historic moment, showing what the Red Heads had shown for almost four decades: women could compete with men.

Despite all of these landmark events, the biggest would be the passing of what has come to be called Title IX. Looking back, we can see that this had a huge impact on women's athletics, but that wasn't the purpose at the time of its derivation. Essentially, President Johnson wanted to clarify aspects of the 1964 Civil Rights Act, an act that didn't give include any prohibitions on gender discrimination in public education and federally assisted programs. Executive Order 11375 prohibited any organizations receiving federal contracts from discriminating against women in matters of hiring and employment.

Shortly thereafter, Bernice Sandler used the executive order to file complaints against the University of Maryland and nearly three hundred other colleges. The fight was joined by the National Organization of Women (NOW) and the Women's Equity Action league (WEAL).

Edith Green was only the second woman from Oregon to be elected to the US House of Representatives and served ten terms from 1955–1974. At the time of her election, she was just one of seventeen women in the House. She worked with Representative Patsy Mink and Senator Birch Bayh to provide women with equal educational opportunities. She was part of a subcommittee on higher education and sat in on relevant congressional hearings. Green invited Bernice Sandler to join these meetings, and along with Mink and Bayh, they came up with the idea of Title IX. The focus was on hiring and employment practices in federally financed institutions. Both Adlai Stevenson in 1956 and John F. Kennedy in 1960 asked Green to second their nominations at the respective Democratic Conventions. Mark Hatfield called Green "the most powerful woman ever to serve in the Congress."

By 1974 there was an awareness that Title IX would impact collegiate athletics by effectively requiring any educational institution to provide for a female sports team where there was an existing male team. This set off a flurry of protest that included various legislative attempts to exclude sports from the Title IX provision, but all of these attempts failed. In 1976 even the NCAA claimed that Title IX was illegal, but the claim, along with several further attempts to remove athletics from under the purview of Title IX, all failed. By 1978 educational institutions were expected and required to comply with the law even though attempts to exempt athletics continued for two decades.

By the end of the seventies, the opportunities for women to play sports, including basketball, in high school and college soared. The time had come.

CHAPTER 13

The Evolving Eighties

● ● ●

Discipline helps you finish a job, and finishing is what
separates excellent work from average work.

—PAT SUMMITT

BY THE TIME THE 1980s rolled, around the landscape had changed dramatically. Title IX was now in full force, giving girls and women the opportunity to play basketball. Not only did that mean there was less novelty to the Red Heads, but at a practical level school and college courts were much more fully occupied with full schedules of games and practices. Moreover, women had made significant strides in status—by the eighties, there were four women leaders of major countries, the United Kingdom, India, Israel, and Pakistan. Not that the battle of the sexes will ever go away, but some of the allure had been lost thanks to the very success of the Red Heads themselves. In addition, with the development of television, the dawning of the personal computer, and the reach of global communications, there were many competing distractions and activities than there were in the 1970s, let alone the 1930s.

Despite all of the above, the Red Heads rolled on in their own inimitable style. Now, however, potential Red Heads were being recruited by colleges from around the country, and so the pool of eligible players expanded in number but shrank in real terms. The Red Heads were now offering players another option after they had completed their college careers and, for one reason or another, not playing in the women's professional league. Around this time the Red Heads fielded a team made up entirely of college graduates.

One of the stars of the early-eighties teams was "Rosie-Red" Ruth Simmons, the team comedienne. Ruth was a student at Western Michigan University majoring in physical education, but after a couple of years, she decided she didn't want to be a teacher. "I wanted to play," she told Celeste Garrett of the Memphis paper the *Commercial Appeal* in an interview in April 1983. "The Red Heads kind of fell into my lap."

Ruth had a great line in the interview:

> If you want to compare us to anyone else, though, we don't mind being compared to the Harlem Globetrotters.
>
> The only difference between them and us is that we play to win first and entertain second.

Ruth's teammates during these years included Janet Grady of Beauville, North Carolina; Mary Benton of Albany, Georgia; Kathy Smith of Durham, North Carolina; Pat Burgess of Byron Center, Michigan; and Marcia Schmidt of Livonia, Mississippi.

The Red Heads continued to amaze the fans and attract publicity. In May 1981 the NBC show *Real People* filmed a game between the Red Heads and a team from Rogersville, Tennessee, calling themselves the Chiefs. There was a crowd of 1,500 who enjoyed all the usual antics, athleticism, and skills of the team, which included six-feet-ten-inch Susan Callahan and legendary Cheryl Clark. The Red Heads won 79–49.

"The ball game turned out to be an evening of delightful entertainment for everyone. Both teams provided humor on the court with the Red Heads using their crafty shooting and pretty smiles to distract the Chiefs," wrote Kathy Rogers in the *Rogersville Review* in May 1981.

As usual the Red Heads surprised their opponents and fans alike with their skills and physical fitness.

"I was really impressed with their ball handling and their conditioning—there was only 6 of them against 16 of us," said Col. Donald J. Hallager of Blytheville Air Force Base. Col. Hallager was on a team called the Flabulous Ones that lost 74–67 in a game played in Gosnell, Arkansas.

As well as playing at home, the Red Heads were still looking for overseas opportunities, especially in the offseason. But it was getting harder to organize such trips. Malaysia turned them down, and after some initial consideration, so did Taipei. An effort was made to reach out to Australia, but the response from Lindsey Gaze, the contact down under, was as follows:

"Women's basketball has progressed dramatically but unfortunately does not draw large enough crowds to enable us to cover the expenses for this type of program."

Despite these apparent rebuffs, the Red Heads were still getting plenty of mail and interest. One unusual request came from an outfit called Above-All Enterprises. This company was a talent agency that represented tall people and wanted to offer their services for some of the taller Red Heads.

However, despite the continued attraction of the Red Heads, forces were building that would lead ultimately to the end of the great adventure. Three main factors contributed to the winding down of the barnstorming team.

First, as already mentioned, there were many more competing attractions. Young people, and especially girls, now had the opportunity to play rather than watch their favorite sports. The Red Heads had been part of the pioneering efforts that meant that instead of just dreaming, girls could now play. In addition, television coverage and programming was both more expansive and ubiquitous. By 1986 Atari had been developing arcade video games for more than a decade, and Pac-Man was already past its prime. More importantly, if you wanted to see women play basketball, there were many colleges and even pro basketball teams that offered highly competitive games in organized leagues.

Secondly, the travel and associated expenses had soared, challenging the economic model that had underpinned the Red Heads organization since its inception. The limo had been traded in for a white van, and it was a challenge keeping motel bills and travel expenses in line with declining revenue. The third factor was that potential players had many other options to either play basketball elsewhere or make considerably more money getting a different sort of job.

Orwell knew that it was only a matter of time before the Red Heads would no longer be economically viable, but he was determined that the team should complete their fiftieth anniversary by playing a full schedule of games in 1986.

Karen Riggs (now Dowty) was one of the last Red Heads recruits. In high school she had been coached by Jack Moore, so she knew all about the Red Heads and had even been to Camp Courage.

"Camp Courage was awesome," said Karen. "It was a wonderful experience that wasn't just about basketball, but about how to get along as friends and teammates. We didn't just play basketball—we swam, played softball, and learned how to bond," said Karen, who was signed right out of high school. At five feet four and with great ball-handling and shooting skills, she made the perfect point guard and team comedienne, even if she was just eighteen.

Karen was an ever-present force during the Red Heads' final season along with stalwarts Joanne Boone, Tammy Elkins, and Tammy Bledsoe. Marsha Schmidt started the season but was later replaced in what became something of a revolving door as a number of younger players, mostly in their late teens, had spells on the road. These included Michelle Pollard, Sherry Marshall, Marla Carroll, and Kelli Horrell.

"We knew that it was getting expensive to keep the team on the road and that there we a lot of competing attractions, but no one knew that this would be the last year. We all wanted to ensure we could finish the season and help Orwell realize his fiftieth-anniversary dream," said Karen.

The Red Heads played in mostly high school venues in front of enthusiastic crowds in fairly full gyms. Compared to the more than 200 games that were played by Red Heads teams in the past (sometimes 3 Red Heads teams playing 600 games in total in a season) the 1986 team played just 121 games.

They won 114 of them.

Toward the end of their final season the Red Heads played a game in North Carolina against a very talented and athletic team of African-American men. These guys had won their league and were determined they were not going to be beaten by a bunch of women.

It was clear that the Red Heads were going to have their work cut out both on and off the floor. Their opponents weren't going to give an inch, and the crowd was waiting to be impressed. When the Red Heads fell behind early and trailed by ten points, the crowd got restive. There were even some boos when one of the girls missed a shot or turned the ball over.

"We were beginning to wonder whether the crowd would ask for their money back," remembers Karen, even after the crowd warmed to the Red Heads' half-time show.

"We hung in there. They weren't giving us an inch, and try as we might we weren't making any inroads into their lead. Gradually, we chipped away, and it came down to the final few seconds. We were down by one point, but they had the ball."

The Red Heads made a defensive stop and got the ball at their end of the court. Bernie called a timeout and drew up the play.

"They were pressuring us all over the court. However, I made a fake and burst down the court. The long inbound pass just evaded the long reach of one of the opponents, and I was able to lay it in at the buzzer for the win," said Karen.

The crowd, who had been subdued up to that point, went wild.

"The crowd was wonderful. They were buying posters and memorabilia, and we were signing autographs all night," said Karen.

Bernie did a good job of managing to keep a group of mostly teenagers in line and in shape. And these weren't 1930s teenagers—they were 1980s teenagers, and there was a difference.

"He pretty much kept us in line," said Karen. But when Orwell came to the games, the girls knew what they had to do.

"Orwell probably came to thirty or so games that year. And each time he did we all redyed our hair—Clairol thirty-three—and made sure we were on top of our game," recalled Karen.

If the culture of the team and the results were similar over their fifty-year playing days, some things changed with the passage of time. In the fifties and even the sixties, mail call was a big deal as the girls anxiously waited for the news from home. By 1986 the girls were calling home every night.

"I called home every night, and my mom in particular was thrilled to hear about the details of the game and my stats, which she faithfully recorded in her book. She mapped where I was playing and everything about the team's performance. And, of course, if we were playing anywhere near my home, my parents and often my older brother would show up," said Karen.

Karen played in thirty-six states in her one year with the Red Heads, but that too marked a difference between the final Red Heads team and earlier versions. In previous decades, and especially the further back you went, the opportunity to travel and see the country was a huge plus, a once-in-a-lifetime opportunity. By the mid-1980s, however, such travel was well within the reaches and expectations of many young people. You could travel the country in more comfort and style than sitting with a group of people in a van for hours at a time.

Karen went to the induction ceremonies of both the Women's Basketball and the Naismith Hall of Fame as well as other reunions.

"Mostly, I like to listen because my stories are nothing compared to the tales I hear from the women who came before me. They were the trailblazers, and I look up to every one of them. They laid the path for the rest of us. It is truly amazing what they did," said Karen.

Fittingly, the last game of the last season was played in Cassville, Missouri. Of course, the Red Heads won. They entertained, they soared—they gave it everything they had.

In some ways, the Red Heads were the victims of their own success. They had helped create the opportunities for women in basketball and sports to the point that they themselves were no longer a curiosity, and they no longer represented a distant vision. They had represented a dream, and now it was a reality.

For the most part the Red Heads' playing days were over. But in so many ways the Red Heads live on, as a unique and special family.

CHAPTER 14

Reunions

● ● ●

You can't live a perfect day without doing something
for someone who will never be able to repay you.

—JOHN WOODEN

IN JULY 1996, THE RED Heads celebrated their sixtieth birthday by having a massive reunion. Players from across the eras and the country descended on Jonesboro, Arkansas. In an article in the *Jonesboro Sun*, Orwell Moore was quoted as saying that he expected 95 percent of the players who were still living to attend. Probably some of those not living attended as well.

The keynote speaker for the Friday-evening banquet was Phyllis Holmes of the Women's Basketball Hall of Fame.

The next evening, July 26, 1996, the Red Heads suited up and played their last game after a ten-year interval. A commemorative game was played against the Walmart All Stars at the Albert Payne gym, which was on the former Caraway High campus, where Orwell Moore began his coaching career. The City of Caraway marked the occasion by declaring it All-American Red Heads Basketball Team Day.

The reunion was so popular that they started to become a regular feature over the next few years and assumed increasing importance. The reunions were often the chance not just for the Red Heads to reminisce and even play but to be honored.

In 1998, for example, the Red Heads were invited to Kanas City, where the NCAA Women's Final Four was taking place. The Women's Basketball Coaches Association was having its seventeenth annual national convention at the same time. The convention is a big deal as coaches from all over the country and from every division and league discuss national and local issues. Many awards and accolades are handed out, and there is a tremendous energy and excitement for the four days of the event, culminating in the Final Four games themselves.

On Saturday, March 28, 1998, at the convention center, Sears sponsored a Salute to the Champions brunch. It featured the Red Heads! The emcee was no less than Robin Roberts, the leading ESPN female announcer and host at the time.

Robin Roberts had a podium in the center of the head tables. There were coaches and basketball elites as far back as the eye could see. Reserved seats were in the front of all the other tables labeled ALL AMERICAN RED HEADS. Then the tribute to the All American Red Heads began. Individual names were called, and players and coaches were recognized with incredible enthusiasm and love. Jolene Ammons, Jessie Banks, Donna Losier, Lynnea Sjoquist, Lynette Sjoquist, Orwell Moore, Lorene Moore, and Pat Overman strolled out to a standing ovation. After the event there were huge lines as literally dozens of people waited to get autographs of the team. It is truly a magical memory. Beth Bass and the Women's Basketball Coaches Association will always have a place in Orwell's and Tammy's hearts for making the event happen.

As if the convention in Kansas City wasn't enough, the following year brought another great reunion and even more recognition.

The Women's Basketball Hall of Fame recognizes both men and women who have advanced the state of women's basketball. It exists to "honor the past, celebrate the present, and promote the future of women's basketball." The Hall of Fame is located in Knoxville, Tennessee, where there was a big following of women's basketball because of the perennial success in the nineties of the Lady Vols University of Tennessee team.

The Hall of Fame was opened in June 1999, and the Red Heads were a big part of the opening. An entire hall is dedicated to the Red Heads, featuring an original Red Heads limousine and memorabilia that spans half a century. There was a rousing and spectacular event that once again recognized the Red Heads' achievements.

The Hall of Fame's thirty-two-thousand-square-foot building hosted many notables and events on that opening weekend. Prominent was Pat Summitt, a famous coach and promoter of women's basketball who coached the University of Tennessee Lady Volunteers. The weekend's activities were topped off with a game between the Washington Mystics and the Houston Comets.

After two consecutive years of joyous celebration and recognition, it seemed inconceivable that the following year had no such event on the schedule. So one was planned. The Millennium celebration was held in Jonesboro, Arkansas, in July of 2000. During the festivities and fun, there was time to honor Phyllis Holmes, director of the Women's Basketball Hall of Fame, and Beth Bass, executive director of the Women's Basketball Coaches Association, at a special brunch.

FIMBA is an organization that promotes basketball competition among "mature" teams. Age groups range from thirty to seventy-five, and competitions are held all over the world.

The International Maxibasketball Federation was created on August 21, 1991. Eight countries signed its foundation, and the first president was Eduardo Rodriguez Lamas from Argentina, now known as the Maxibasketball creator. The term "maxibasketball" was created to recognize the maturity of the players.

The sixth FIMBA Maxibasketball championships were held in Oregon in 2010. Ruben Rodriguez Lamas, FIMBA president, invited the Red Heads to participate and "receive the recognition due you."

The invitation continued: "The relevance of your story and the legacy you left as female athletes and basketball players needs to be told. Our tournament will allow your story to be shared with athletes around the globe."

The president stated that it was FIMBA's goal to give "master basketball players an opportunity to enjoy the game at the highest level with teams from all over the world."

The letter concluded: "We would be sincerely honored to have the All-American Red Heads participate in the Awards ceremony for the women's championship. Your presence would exemplify the global spirit of athletes and is an important chapter in basketball's history."

This letter was received shortly after Orwell Moore had passed away. Of course, the Red Heads were going!

The exhibition game was indeed played the following year. Many Red Heads showed up to play (it was twenty-three years since the Red Heads had played their last competitive game), so they all definitely qualified as maxibasketball players.

Tammy Harrison remembers it well.

"The people of Cottage Grove invited us into their beautiful town. They hosted picnics, banquets, a media event, and a basketball game. They furnished cheerleaders and uniforms as well as warm fans. The fans were from the area and from other countries. The region is a combination of beautiful sites that are hidden within driving distance. I would like to thank Pete Barrell, Sue Harshbarger, and Melinda Thompson for their leadership roles in allowing us to have such an immeasurably wonderful week."

As for the game itself, it was played against the Portland Trailblazer alumni. Tammy recalled the following:

"They were extremely wonderful men to play against. The game was played by a group of women, most of whom said that they could not run up and down the court to play. When they put on the uniform, they all decided they could do it. It was hard to get all the players in. I had to worry about getting them injured. Although, they didn't seem to recall that could happen. Brenda O'Bryan Koester, Kay O'Bryan Burk, and Lynn Holt Thomas stole the half-time show by doing routines that they did back in the day. One of the highlights of the game was when Jackie Kurtsinger, who started the week needing a cane to get around, handed her cane off and made a shot under the goal."

Once a Red Head, always a Red Head, even when you're turning gray.

The All American Red Heads have been honored at multiple WNBA games and at the Big East championship games.

CHAPTER 15

A Family Affair

● ● ●

The real Red Heads were like a family. Each team like a
family unit, sharing, caring, and looking at their teammates
through their hearts and not through their eyes.

—ORWELL MOORE

BRENDA O'BRYAN (NOW KOESTER) WAS one of the few married girls whom Orwell Moore accepted into the Red Heads family, and he was sure glad he did.

Brenda grew up with two sisters and two brothers and spent a lot of her childhood playing against the boys in her backyard in the small town of Cairo, Missouri. The population there was 199, which happens to be a special number for Brenda and the Red Heads. She starred as a high school player, and in her senior year the team went undefeated, and she averaged twenty-eight points per game.

"That year, more people came to watch the girls' team than the boys'," Brenda remembers. But this was before Title IX, and there was nowhere to play college ball after high school.

One day Brenda was playing softball down in Louisiana, and her athleticism impressed one of the opposing players, Pauline Barbo. Pauline was playing for the Red Heads and after the game spoke to Brenda. When Pauline mentioned basketball, Brenda told her that the game was her passion. Before long, Brenda had been invited to Camp Courage. There was a potential problem, however. Though still young, Brenda was married to a guy in the air force who was about to be posted overseas.

"I come from a very small town and was very shy. So I was very nervous getting on that bus to Holley Springs on my way to Camp Courage," recalled Brenda. "When I got off the bus and there was no one there to meet me, I wanted to turn around and go home. If a bus had come along I probably would have done just that."

Fortunately, a bus didn't come along before she was met and taken to camp.

Brenda did well at camp, and it wasn't long before Orwell called her into his office.

"I like what I see. But I don't usually take married women because they don't stay. I would like you to play for us, but if you have to call and ask your husband, then it won't work," said Orwell.

"Where do I sign?" said Brenda.

Brenda started every game as a rookie, typically playing forward. She was a stellar ball handler and shooter with a wicked hook shot. She said she learned a lot from watching Jolene Ammons's juggling acts. "I thought that was very cool," said Brenda, who tried to emulate her idol.

In three years with the Red Heads, Brenda scored 10,017 points, a 15-points-per-game average, and her team won 585 of the 644 games she played. And that brings up that special number—199. The last year Brenda played, the team went an incredible 199–6.

"Jack Moore was a heck of a coach," said Brenda, who also was briefly coached by Ben Overman and Wilbur Coggins.

Her most memorable trip was to Alaska.

"We were in a town that had just one truck, and the team rode around in the back of that pickup. We played forty-four games in thirty days."

You couldn't be shy and a Red Head, and being on the road with the team and being the center of attention brought Brenda out of her shell.

"When I got home at the end of my first season, my mom couldn't believe I was the same person," said Brenda.

At Camp Courage the next year, Brenda met Lynn Holst, and they quickly became friends. The problem was that they were scheduled to be on different Red Heads teams. They came up with a plan. If they could develop a new routine together, perhaps they could both make the same team. In the heat of the summer they worked hard on developing a new routine, two players, each dribbling two balls—the double dribble. When they perfected their act after hours and hours of practice, they showed it to the boss. Orwell was impressed.

"We'll have to have you guys on the same team," said the boss. And that's how the double-dribble act was developed and how Brenda and Lynn got to play together.

The next year, sister Kay, five years younger than Brenda and known affectionately as KK, joined the Red Heads. She looked up to her elder sister.

"The whole family was excited about Brenda playing for the Red Heads. My dad would tell anyone who would listen that his daughter played professional basketball. Even my grandparents couldn't stop talking about it and went to any games that were played in Missouri and even Illinois," said Kay.

Despite the five-year age difference, Brenda and Kay had played on the same women's softball team. Brenda had been the pitcher and Kay the catcher, even though she was only in the seventh grade. However, when she got to the Red Heads, Kay was scheduled to play on a different traveling team from Brenda, and they were thus separated. And by now Brenda was separated from her husband.

"We were very young and both wanted different things out of life," said Brenda.

Brenda feels blessed that she had the opportunity to play with the Red Heads. And she and sister KK still play. They have been to every reunion and always put on an amazing dribbling, shooting, and juggling act, even now, forty years after they played their last games for the Red Heads. To keep in shape, Brenda plays ball with her grandchildren.

"We play H-O-R-S-E and even a little one-on-one," said Brenda, whose children excelled at the game. Jason, six feet seven inches, played pro ball in France, and daughter Jamie was a star in college. Brenda's three grandsons Jalen, Trey, and Brendan and her granddaughter Kayla are now playing ball, and two have made it onto their respective high school varsity teams as freshmen. Kay also plays ball with her grandson Eli, just four, who loves to watch his grandmother do her juggling tricks.

Kay played one season under Coach Charlotte Adams. "We both agree now that she should have been tougher on me," said Kay, who decided to return home after one season on the road. But a year later, on a visit to see a Red Heads game in Missouri, she felt nostalgic and wanted to get back out on the floor. She talked to Orwell Moore, who had her signed up and back on the road with the traveling team within forty-eight hours.

The following year, the 1975–76 season, Kay featured in the "College Edition" team, which consisted of players who all had gone to college and benefitted somewhat from the newly implemented Title IX. Despite not having gone to college and being the youngest player, Kay was made captain. She knew the Red Heads way of doing things even if she was just twenty. That was a lot of responsibility, especially on one occasion when the Red Heads' limo broke down in Missouri. Coach Les Wren had to stay with the car while Kay rented a van and drove the team to the game, where she acted as announcer, coach, and sales manager.

Kay (now Kay Burk) moved to Fort Madison, Iowa, in 1990 and has been involved in coaching at the high school level for many years. Recently, her basketball career took a new twist. Her daughter, Krisha, was born with some developmental difficulties that really prevented her from playing sports even though she was a more-than-willing helper at Mom's practices and games. After visiting a Special Olympics game last year, Krisha said she wanted to play. Of course, Kay helped out with the coaching, and Krisha, at thirty-five, finally got to play in a competitive game. She scored four points and realized a dream.

Kay lives two and a half hours away from Brenda, but when it's reunion time she heads west to her sister's, and the two of them sharpen up their routine for a week or so before the reunion.

"Each year we say we're going to do it 'one more time,'" said Brenda. The O'Bryan family tradition doesn't stop with Kay and Brenda. Dad, who was six feet five, didn't play much organized ball but encouraged all his children, and four of them excelled at basketball. As well as Brenda and Kay, his two sons, Danny and Randy, both played in college. Dad spent a lot of time watching his kids play and hardly missed a game. Whenever the Red Heads were even close to Missouri, Mom and Dad—and grandparents—went to cheer them on.

Mom is a story in her own right. She was a softball player, but she was also the biggest Red Heads fan. Wilma went to every reunion and is known by the other Red Heads simply as "Mom." When her husband died in 2000, Wilma was still determined to go, despite declining health. She was helped on these trips by another daughter, Kenna. Brenda and Kay's big sister was always a huge cheerleader and fan of both her sisters and the Red Heads. Her presence at the reunions, where she often assisted her mother, as well as her support, has made Kenna part of the Red Heads' family, too.

Wilma made the long trip to Eugene, Oregon, in 2010 for the FIMBA championships even though she was in a wheelchair and needed a lot of assistance, which Kenna gladly provided. Wilma was so passionate about the Red Heads that Orwell even gave her a special award—the Heritage Family Award.

Wilma was so excited when she heard that the Red Heads had been inducted into the Naismith Memorial Basketball Hall of Fame in 2012. Despite her failing health, Wilma declared, "I'm going to that ceremony." Regrettably, Wilma's health prevented her from going, but she proudly displayed a banner in her front yard to welcome her two daughters home from the induction ceremony.

Wilma passed away a few months later in December 2012 at the age of eighty-three. She treasured the special family award that Orwell had so thoughtfully given her. She represented the spirit of many parents and family members who passionately supported their children and siblings as they changed a sport and the perception of women.

For Orwell and Lorene, the Red Heads team wasn't just a family business; it was also the business of family. Orwell always emphasized that fact and made sure that tight family bonds were the strength of the team and the core of the organization. A team is a family, and a family should be a team.

"I was always totally amazed about Orwell's ability to remember so many things. The man must have had a photographic memory. In particular, he remembered the names of all the players' family members and always stressed the importance of close family bonds," said Brenda.

The support and opportunity to excel at their passions that Brenda and KK received from their family was the norm for any girl fortunate enough to play for the Red Heads. And like many other Red Heads, Brenda and KK have paid it forward to their families and future generations.

It will soon be time for another family reunion.

Brenda and KK are getting ready.

CHAPTER 16

The Dream Is Realized

Tammy Moore Harrison

*Things turn out best for the people who make
the best of the way things turn out.*

—JOHN WOODEN

THE DREAM OF BEING INDUCTED in to the Naismith Memorial Basketball
Hall of Fame was just out of sight for my parents. My mother passed away
in 2002, and my father in 2009. He started putting together his ideas for a
book, planning to name it *Just out of Sight*. Although he did not finish the
book, the name seemed to fit the information at the time of its inception.
He truly believed that one day the Red Heads would be members of the
elite group known as inductees of the Naismith Memorial Basketball Hall
of Fame—the pinnacle of the basketball world. Yet he seemed to know it
would not happen in his lifetime.

The Red Heads were nominated to the Naismith Memorial Basketball
Hall of Fame in 2010 but didn't make the cut. Still it was an honor to get
a letter saying that the team was in the final running. In 2012, I was noti-
fied that the team would be inducted. I couldn't tell anyone until it was
announced at the Final Four in New Orleans. It was so hard to keep it
quiet. I felt the need to scream it out, and following the wishes of the Hall

of Fame was hard. When I thought about the people who had been such a great part of the success of the team but had passed, it sorrowed me that they could not be there. They would miss all of the great hoopla.

I would represent the team. It was an honor. I felt great pressure to live up to all expectations with my speeches, at which I am not a pro. The fact that I would be in the company of global icons and on video only ramped up the pressure. I am thankful to my friend Matt Zysing for helping me add some flair to my words.

After meeting the fellow inductees, I knew why it had taken so long to be a part of the big hall. Then my answer, Ecclesiastes 3:1, states, "There is a time for everything and a season for every activity under the heavens."

The 2012 inductees included the All American Red Heads, Lidia Alexeva, Don Barksdale, Mel Daniels, Phil Knight, Katrina McClain, Reggie Miller, Don Nelson, Hank Nichols, Ralph Sampson, Chet Walker, and Jamal Wilkes. They were very accepting of the first women's team to be inducted, as were the others. They were truly a humble and deserving group of men and women. All of the people involved treated me and all the other players with warm, welcoming arms, as did the fans.

Then it was time to go on stage.

CHAPTER 17

The Ultimate Prize

Tammy Harrison

● ● ●

Champions are not the ones who always win races—champions are
the ones who get out there and try. And try harder the next time.
And even harder the next time. "Champion" is a state of mind. They
are devoted. They compete to best themselves as much if not more
than they compete to best others. Champions are not just athletes.

—SIMON SINEK

I WAS COMING TO THE critical part of my acceptance speech at the Naismith
Basketball Hall of Fame induction of the Red Heads in 2012.

The audience had been generous in their applause, warm in their
welcome, and authentic in their appreciation. Some of them knew the
history that has unfolded in the prior pages of this book, and some
didn't. However, even if they didn't know the details, they knew the
significance of the Red Heads. They knew that Ole and Doyle and my
mom and dad weren't just fielding a basketball team—they were making history. This wasn't just about basketballs and hoops but perception
and respect.

"Ole and Doyle broke the ice and gave women a future in sports."

It takes courage as well as vision and even a little audacity to step outside the box, especially in a public arena.

"For all those who dared to challenge the status quo, this honor is for you."

I asked for patience as I prepared to talk about my parents and their contribution to the Red Heads legend. I paused, momentarily overcome by emotion, as I thought of them both looking down on this moment. I couldn't praise them highly enough.

"Orwell and Lorene dedicated their lives to the Red Heads and their families. Thank you both for promoting, loving, living, and respecting the game of basketball."

I could almost see them both smiling as the crowd burst into applause.

"Thank you for providing a passion and business sense that tore the roof off the limitations."

As you have read, the Red Heads were trailblazers, pioneers who inspired women and defied the expectations of the time. They helped create a new image and perception of a woman. She could now be an athlete who could compete with men.

"The Red Heads paved the way for much greater opportunities for women in sports at all levels."

It's easy in hindsight to see the natural progression of things, to see how one step led to the next, and to the next, until a small grain of sand turned into a beach, or an outrageous idea into an accepted norm. Hindsight minimizes the effort, courage, and insight that are needed to get a ball—even a basketball—rolling.

"Without taking that momentous first step, women's basketball would not be where it is today, and we would not be here to accept this honor."

As I came to the conclusion of my speech, I could almost see my father. I could hear him and almost touch him. In many respects his life had been lived for this very moment. This precise second in time was the realization of his hopes and dreams. It was his Everest.

"My dad never gave up the idea that the All American Red Heads would someday reach his goal of being enshrined into the Naismith

Hall of Fame. He knew that as the definitive honor in the game of basketball."

I finished my speech, and all of us on that stage were greeted with a standing ovation. We were the All American Red Heads, proud inductees into the 2012 class of the Naismith Basketball Hall of Fame.

CHAPTER 18

All American Red Heads Players and Coaches

● ● ●

1930s
Gene Langerman
Gladys Lommier Putney
Hazel Smith
Hazel Vickers Cone
Helene Walls
Jean Langerman
Jo Langerman
Kay Kirkpatrick Phillips
Lela Blue Lommier
Lera Dunford
Louise White
Myrtle Wallace Frost
Nota Lea McCain Brunson
Peggy Lawson Surface
Ruth Osbon
Torchy Blasch

Coach: Wilbur Surface

1940s
Alice "Peaches" Hatcher
Allegra Winters
Beth Bohannon

Beth Lively
Betty Arends Tamas
Betty Bradshaw Owen
Billie Thurbur
Bonnie Buell
Charline Greene
Danny Daniels
Eloise "Purkey" Malaska
Evelyn McGee Turner
Florence Boyles
Gene Love McHughes
Hazel Reynolds
Hazel Walker
Johnny Farley
Juanita Coleman
Judith Matlock
Lorene "Butch" Moore
Lorene Milligan Atwell
Louise White
Mabel Matlock
Marcella Staggs
Margie Arends Hannaman
Mary Ann Martin Leake
Mayonne Moore
Myrtle Wallace Frost
Orwell "Red" Moore
Pauline Smedley
Phyllis Meyers
Phyllis White
Willa Faye "Red" Mason
Ruby Hayes
Ruth Haines Helleland
Ruth Haynes
Toby McGee

Vinia Hobbs
Virginia Posey
Wilson Turner

Coaches: Orwell Moore, Wilson Turner, Bernard Cowden, Hazel Walker

1950s
Alice Hammond Kilgore
Ann Taft
Annette Binkley
Barbara Eyde Lovett
Barbara Wells Gwinn
Bessie Shelton Elliot
Betty Bradshaw
Betty Jo Bollinger Simpson
Bonie Gilliland
Bonnie Buel
Charlene Green
Dean Lorrance
Dody Petersen
Dolores Peterson Clack
Dorsey Anderson Dinkla
Ella Cross Wright
Emily Cowden
Emogean Shelten Carter
Esther Taylor Sanderson
Eunice Wilkening
Fran Saunders
Ginny Morris Merril
Glen Green
Harlene Walls
Herman Keith (driver)
Jackie Bray
Jackie Krutsinger

Jackie Wrage Zitiau
Jackie Wranger
Jan Hardy
Janie Green
Jeannine "Jeep" Gogel Doe
Jerry Holt
Jessie Banks
Jessie Paul Shelton (driver)
Jo Darrow
Jo Underwood Hightower
Joanne Foster
Judith Matlock
Justine Glover Arthur
Katherine Pittcock Clack
Katie Ingrahm Watson
Linda Kafer Mitchell
Lois Glover Sitler
Lorene "Butch" Moore
Lorene Milligan Atwell
Loretta Thompson
Mabel Matlock
Mamie Holder Lynch
Margaret O'Neal
Marie Reynolds Boggess
Mary Moore
Myrtle Wallace Frost
Nellie Marlow Hudgen
Oma Jean Barnes
Patty Peterson
Patty Woody Burton
Red Eyde
Red Holder
Retha Carter Goodson
Reva Henry

Ruby Hayes
Ruth Harms
Sammy Autry Gordon
Shelby Tedder Faulkner
Shelvia "Shorty" Johnson
Shirley "Trooper" Howard
Shirley Bray Taylor
Sylvia Johnson
Tommie Woods
Velma Barnett Gray
Wilburn Coggins (driver)
Willa Faye "Red" Mason
Zethel Keith Mathews

Coaches: Orwell Moore, Glenn Green, Red Mason, Dean Lorrance, Willa Faye "Red" Mason, Lorene "Butch" Moore, Ben Overman, Wilburn Coggins

1960s
Aaronette Efling Housley
Alice Washington Dockins
Ann Cragger
Barbara Baty Hicks
Barbara Shrable
Becky Birtcher Thompson
Becky Harp Pritchett
Bessie Shelton
Betty Everett
Betty Springer Wonka
Beverly Turley Douglas
Brenda Hubbard Watson
Brenda Moon Davis
Brenda Ragan Nalpa

Carolyn Gooch Hix
Carolyn Grantham Booth
Carolyn Linzay
Catherine Jones Deweese
Cathy Jones
Charlotte Adams
Dana Granger Mahan
Debbie Smith Loftice
Delphia Allen Hemphires
Donna Granger Mahan
Donna Losier
Doris Jones
Ella Cross
Eunice Wilkening
Georgia Washington Norris
Glenda Ledbetter
Helen Daughdrill
Jan Hardy
Jana Giles
Janet Cox
Jeanne Ohleman
Jolene Ammons
Joni Phillips
Joyce Eastman
Joyce Webster
Judith Coghlan Lewis
Judy Cameron
Judy Eifling Flettcher
Kathy Holbrook
Kay Ferguson
Kay Shinal Craig
Larry Emison
Lavella Polston McWilliams

Linda Chandler Kidd
Linda Mitchell Steed
Linda Shanks
Lois Glover Sitler
Loretta Thompson
Margaret McNeil Hansmann
Marie Daughdrill
Martha Olsen
Mary Bennett
Mary Carpenter
Mary Emison Hester
Mary Hounsell
Mary Parsons
Mickey Gay
Mickey Hendricks Childress
Pam MacAnally
Pat Rakowitz
Pat Rimer Overman
Pat Vaugh Johnson
Patricia "Watusie" DeRoche Hymel
Patty Eubank
Pauline Barbo
Peggy Padget Baugher
Rebecca Birtcher
Reva Henry
Rosali Kashmitter Friburger
Sandra Bishop Satcher
Sandy Mann
Sharon Glenn Helterbrant
Shelby Tedder Faulkner
Sheryl Wood Borgman
Shirley Beckman Cheatum
Sue Dawson
Teresa Bergeron

Tex Glover
Theda Van winkle Ely
Wilda Kelley Clettenburg

Coaches: Ben Overman, Jack Moore, Richard Gray, Chuck Plummer, Larry Emison, Glenn Green

1970s
Annette Calvin
April Jenson
Barbara Hostert
Beverly Searcy Lyle
Brenda O'Bryan Kostner
Carolyn Gooch Hix
Carolyn Reeves
Carolyn Williamson
Carolyn Wooldridge Williams
Charlotte Adams
Cheryl Clark
Cheryl Wood
Cindy Laliberte Nelson
Cindy Roybal
Connie Howe
Debbie Parashak
Denise Maurals Doucette
Diane Martinson
Donna "Spanky" Losier
Donna See
Emma Batness Eute
Frank Roy
Gail Marks
Glenda Hall McClain
Gretchen Pinz Hyink
Gwen Reed

James Moore (driver)
Jana Giles
Jane Hounsell Stotts
Janet Grady
Jeanne Ohleman
Jewell Hair
Jolene Ammons
Joni Phillips
Joy Ribitsky
Judy Babcock
Karen Logan
Karen Milner Coggins
Katherine Smith
Kathy Jones Heck
Kathy McCall Smith
Kathy Tipton
Kay Smith O'Brien
Kay O'Bryan Burk
LaRa Gibbs
Linda Jones
Linda Kafer Cain
Linda Shanks
Lisa Livingston
Lois Glover
Lynn Holt Thomas
Lynnea Sjoquist
Lynnette Sjoquist
Marcia Adams
Marilyn Nelson
Marsha Tate
Mary Benton
Mary Hounsell
Mary Leasure
Mary Parsons

Martha Hix
Nancy Malone
Pam Rowlett
Pat Rimer Overman
Patricia Dyer
Patricia DaRoche Hymel
Patty Bruce
Paula Allbritton
Paula Haverstick Pollock
Pauline Barbo
Phillip Brooks (driver)
Rhonda Waters Boatwright
Ruth Simmons
Sally Leyse
Sandy Crist
Sherri Mattson
Sheryl Wood Borgman
Sue Branham Kohler
Sue Whitten Ford
Susan Callahan
Teresa Bergeron
Tina Treat Johnson
Trudy Babcock Kutz
Vicky Halbery
Wanda England Lewis
William Vaughn (driver)

Coaches: Cheryl Clark, Charlotte Adams, Jack Moore, Ben Overman, Wilbur Coggins, Lethco Wrenn, Glenda Hall, Gwen Reed, Jolene Ammons, Rhonda Waters, Bill Stotts

1980s
April Jenson
Denise Levy

Donna Losier
Donna See
Gail Marks
Gwen Reed
Janet Grady
Jo Ann Boone
Karen Riggs Dowty
Kathy Smith O'Brien
Kelli Harrison
Kelli Horrell Harris
Lisa Livingston
Marla Carroll
Marsha Schmidt
Mary Benton
Mary Prater
Mechelle Pollard Weyer
Pat Burgess
Pat Dyer
Paula Gregg
Penny Prater
Ruth Simmons
Sandy Crist
Sherri Marshall Wutherman
Susan Callahan Cooper
Tammy Bledsoe
Tammy Elkins

Coaches: Cheryl Clark, Ruth Simmons, Orwell Moore, Burnie Moore

1990s
Played a few games in the '90s—under Coach Orwell Moore
Coached the last two game the team played – Tammy Moore Harrison

Angie Reed
Christi Pack
Jamie Pace
Julie Boyles
Karen Riggs Dowty
Kim Wright
Missy Wright
Paula Lincoln Gregg
Sandra Berry
Sonia Schoolfield

Special thanks to Hailey Faulkner Vaughn for her help preparing the information. Along with Madge Taylor and Jolene Ammons.

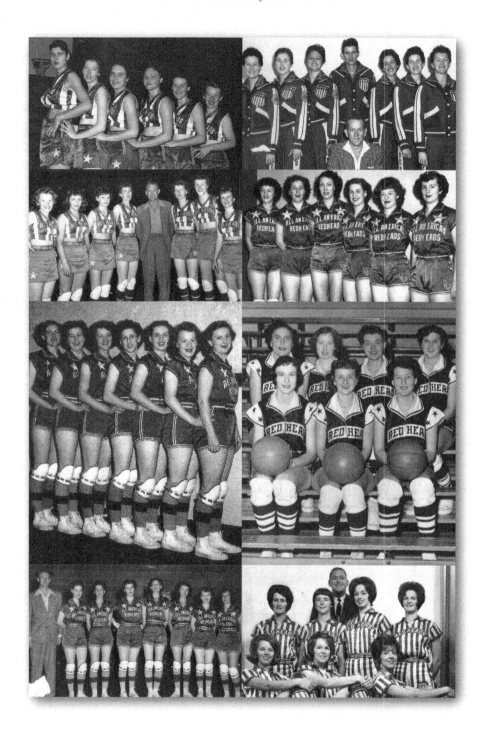

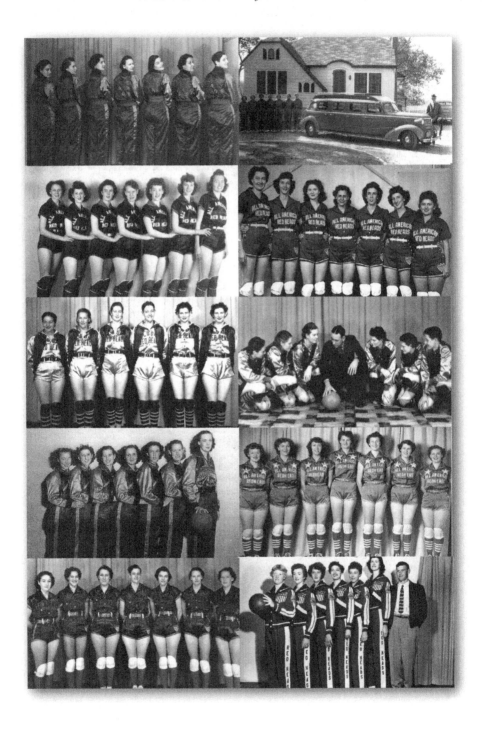

Orwell Moore

Orwell "Red" Moore was a winning basketball coach on both the high school and professional levels. He was the winningest coach in the history of the All-American Red Heads, winning 1,813 games and losing 303. He was a graduate of Arkansas College (Arkansas State University) in Jonesboro, Arkansas, where he acquired a bachelor of science and education degree with minors in English, physical education, and social studies.

He served as the national baseball commissioner in the State of Arkansas as well as coaching baseball, which was his first love. His dream as a young boy was to play for the St. Louis Cardinals, but that would not come to be after he was stricken with tuberculosis. He held an athletic training certificate. He also served as both an Arkansas semipro men's baseball commissioner and a coach within this league. He even spent time coaching a women's AAU softball team.

He had three children—Linda Kaye, Tammy Jayne, and Burnice Orwell Jr.; three grandchildren—Cassie Nelson, Colby Harrison, and Travis Harrison; and three great-grandchildren—Zephyr Rigaud, Trevor, and Alissa Harrison

Tammy Moore Harrison

Tammy Moore Harrison did not have a school team to play for until her junior year in high school. However, she attended Camp Courage and trained all summer during her youth. Title IX brought new opportunities, and the town was forced to form a girls' team on which Tammy played. She played one year of junior college and then obtained a bachelor of science in education (emphasis in physical education) and a master's degree in education. She has taught a variety of subjects, sports, and grade levels and coached a diversity of sports throughout her thirty-three years as an educator.

She coached the last two games the Red Heads played. Also she is the current owner of the team.

Tammy has a daughter, Cassie Brooke Nelson, who played college volleyball at Nichol State Louisiana in Thibeaux, Louisiana; a son, Colby Kips Harrison, who is now playing college basketball at Louisiana State University in Alexandria, Louisiana; and a stepson, Travis Leigh Harrison, who's married to wife Anna. Tammy also has three grandchildren, Trevor, Zephyr, and Alissa, and has been married to her husband, John K. Harrison, for twenty-three years.

Howard J. Rankin, PhD

Howard had a long career in psychology before switching to a full-time writing career. He has written ten books under his own name, including the best-selling *Inspired to Lose*. He has also coauthored or ghostwritten more than thirty books in such areas as neuroscience, self-development, business, memoir, and sports. You can find out more about Howard at www.psychologywriter.com.

Made in the USA
Coppell, TX
04 February 2020